Better Homes and Gardens®

Fast-Fixin'
Diet
Recipes

Our seal assures you that every recipe in *Fast-Fixin' Diet Recipes*
has been tested in the Better Homes and Gardens® Test Kitchen.
This means that each recipe is practical and reliable,
and meets our high standards of taste appeal.

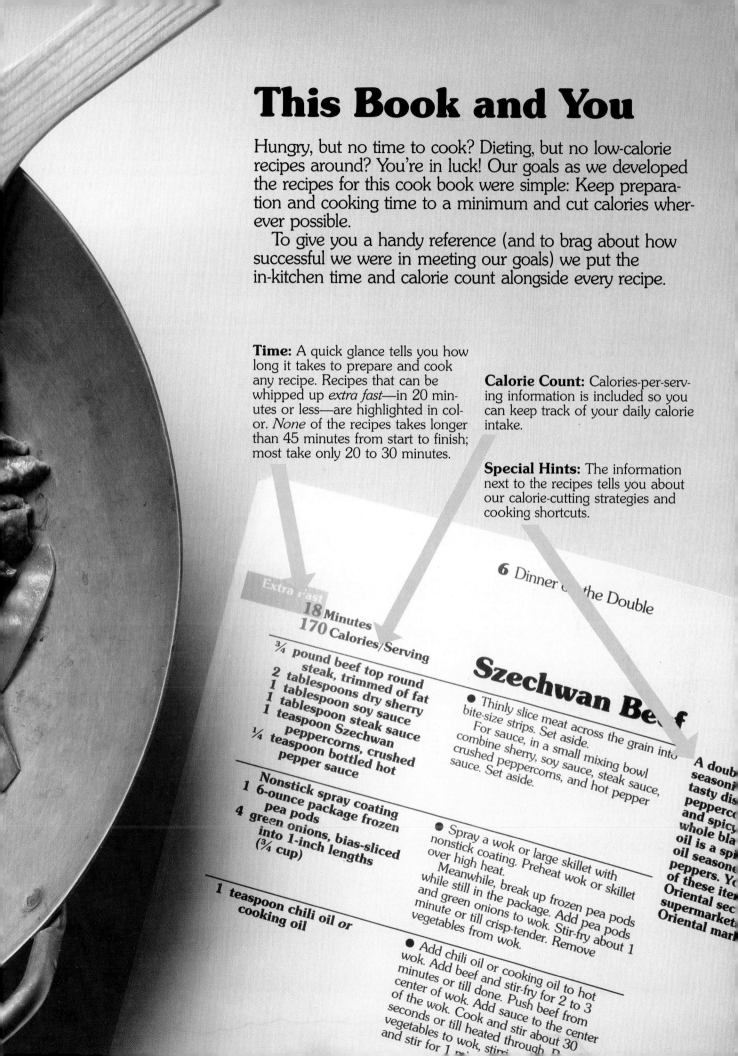

This Book and You

Hungry, but no time to cook? Dieting, but no low-calorie recipes around? You're in luck! Our goals as we developed the recipes for this cook book were simple: Keep preparation and cooking time to a minimum and cut calories wherever possible.

To give you a handy reference (and to brag about how successful we were in meeting our goals) we put the in-kitchen time and calorie count alongside every recipe.

Time: A quick glance tells you how long it takes to prepare and cook any recipe. Recipes that can be whipped up *extra fast*—in 20 minutes or less—are highlighted in color. *None* of the recipes takes longer than 45 minutes from start to finish; most take only 20 to 30 minutes.

Calorie Count: Calories-per-serving information is included so you can keep track of your daily calorie intake.

Special Hints: The information next to the recipes tells you about our calorie-cutting strategies and cooking shortcuts.

Extra fast

18 Minutes
170 Calories/Serving

6 Dinner on the Double

Szechwan Beef

¾ pound beef top round steak, trimmed of fat
2 tablespoons dry sherry
1 tablespoon soy sauce
1 tablespoon steak sauce
1 teaspoon Szechwan peppercorns, crushed
¼ teaspoon bottled hot pepper sauce

● Thinly slice meat across the grain into bite-size strips. Set aside. For sauce, in a small mixing bowl combine sherry, soy sauce, steak sauce, crushed peppercorns, and hot pepper sauce. Set aside.

Nonstick spray coating
1 6-ounce package frozen pea pods
4 green onions, bias-sliced into 1-inch lengths (¾ cup)

● Spray a wok or large skillet with nonstick coating. Preheat wok or skillet over high heat. Meanwhile, break up frozen pea pods while still in the package. Add pea pods and green onions to wok. Stir-fry about 1 minute or till crisp-tender. Remove vegetables from wok.

1 teaspoon chili oil or cooking oil

● Add chili oil or cooking oil to hot wok. Add beef and stir-fry for 2 to 3 minutes or till done. Push beef from center of wok. Add sauce to the center of the wok. Cook and stir about 30 seconds or till heated through. Return vegetables to wok, stir and stir for 1 m...

A doub
seasoni
tasty dis
pepperco
and spicy
whole bla
oil is a sp
oil seasone
peppers. Yo
of these iter
Oriental sec
supermarket
Oriental mar

18 Minutes
170 Calories/Serving

Szechwan Beef

¾ **pound beef top round steak, trimmed of fat**
2 **tablespoons dry sherry**
1 **tablespoon soy sauce**
1 **tablespoon steak sauce**
1 **teaspoon Szechwan peppercorns, crushed**
¼ **teaspoon bottled hot pepper sauce**

● Thinly slice meat across the grain into bite-size strips. Set aside.
   For sauce, in a small mixing bowl combine sherry, soy sauce, steak sauce, crushed peppercorns, and hot pepper sauce. Set aside.

A double dose of Oriental seasonings peps up this tasty dish. Szechwan peppercorns are fragrant and spicy, but milder than whole black pepper. Chili oil is a spicy, red-colored oil seasoned with chili peppers. You'll find both of these items in the Oriental sections of larger supermarkets or in Oriental markets.

   Nonstick spray coating
1 **6-ounce package frozen pea pods**
4 **green onions, bias-sliced into 1-inch lengths (¾ cup)**

● Spray a wok or large skillet with nonstick coating. Preheat wok or skillet over high heat.
   Meanwhile, break up frozen pea pods while still in the package. Add pea pods and green onions to wok. Stir-fry about 1 minute or till crisp-tender. Remove vegetables from wok.

1 **teaspoon chili oil *or* cooking oil**

● Add chili oil or cooking oil to hot wok. Add beef and stir-fry for 2 to 3 minutes or till done. Push beef from center of wok. Add sauce to the center of the wok. Cook and stir about 30 seconds or till heated through. Return vegetables to wok, stirring to coat. Cook and stir for 1 minute more. Serves 4.

Stir-frying is a great way to cook most kinds of meat. But how can you be sure the meat will be tender, not tough? Part of the secret is the way you cut the meat before cooking begins. Slice it very thinly across the grain for optimum tenderness.
   First, if you have time, partially freeze the meat so it's easier to slice—about 45 minutes should do it. Then, hold a sharp knife or cleaver at a 45-degree angle to the cutting board while you thinly slice the meat. Cut any large slices into bite-size pieces.

Slender Stroganoff

25 Minutes
270 Calories/Serving

1 cup quick-cooking rice
1 8-ounce carton plain low-fat yogurt
4 teaspoons cornstarch
1 teaspoon sugar
1 teaspoon instant beef bouillon granules
¾ pound beef top round steak, trimmed of fat

● Cook rice according to package directions. Set aside.
   Meanwhile, in a small mixing bowl stir together yogurt, cornstarch, sugar, bouillon granules, ⅓ cup *water,* ¼ teaspoon *salt,* and ¼ teaspoon *pepper.* Set aside.
   Thinly slice meat across the grain into bite-size strips. Set aside.

Nonstick spray coating
1 medium onion, chopped (½ cup)
½ teaspoon bottled minced garlic *or* ⅛ teaspoon garlic powder

● Spray a large skillet with nonstick coating. Preheat skillet over medium heat. Add onion and garlic. Cook and stir till tender but not brown. Remove onion and garlic from skillet.

1 teaspoon cooking oil
2 tablespoons dry sherry
1 4-ounce can sliced mushrooms, drained

● Add oil to hot skillet. Add beef and cook and stir for 2 to 3 minutes or till tender. Push beef from center of skillet. Stir yogurt mixture and add it to center of skillet. Cook and stir till thickened and bubbly. Add sherry and cook and stir 2 minutes more. Stir in onion, garlic, and mushrooms. Heat through. Serve over hot cooked rice. Makes 4 servings.

You're gonna love our slimmed-down stroganoff! Calorie-cutting tactics include choosing lean meat, cooking with nonstick spray coating, and using low-fat yogurt, not sour cream. And although stroganoff is traditionally served over egg noodles, our version calls for fat- and cholesterol-free rice.

Peppered Steak

23 Minutes
210 Calories/Serving

2 teaspoons whole black pepper
1 1-pound beef flank steak

● Coarsely crack black pepper. Sprinkle *half* of the pepper over steak. Rub pepper into meat, pressing with your hands. Turn steak over. Rub remaining pepper into other side of meat.

Mustard Sauce (see recipe, right)

● Place steak on the unheated rack of a broiler pan. Broil 3 to 4 inches from the heat for 8 to 10 minutes or to desired doneness, turning once. Thinly slice meat diagonally across the grain. Spoon Mustard Sauce over beef slices. Serves 4.

Mustard Sauce: Dissolve 1 teaspoon *instant beef bouillon granules* in ¼ cup *dry sherry.* Add 1 cup sliced fresh *mushrooms* and ½ cup thinly sliced *green onion.* Cook, uncovered, till vegetables are tender. Stir 2 teaspoons *all-purpose flour* and 2 teaspoons *prepared or Dijon-style mustard* into ⅓ cup *plain low-fat yogurt.* Add to vegetable mixture. Cook and stir till thickened and bubbly, then cook and stir 1 minute more.

Lime-Sauced Chicken

2 tablespoons margarine *or* butter **4 boned skinless chicken breast halves (about 1 pound total)**	● In a medium skillet melt margarine or butter. Add chicken breasts to skillet and cook over medium-high heat about 10 minutes or till lightly browned and no longer pink, turning once. Remove chicken from skillet, reserving the pan juices. Keep chicken warm.
1 medium lime	● Meanwhile, use a vegetable peeler to remove peel from lime. Cut peel into thin strips and set aside. Squeeze juice from *half* of the lime and set aside (you should have about 1 tablespoon juice).
¾ cup apple juice *or* apple cider **2 teaspoons cornstarch** **1 teaspoon instant chicken bouillon granules** **¼ teaspoon dried mint *or* ¾ teaspoon finely chopped fresh mint**	● For sauce, in a small mixing bowl stir together apple juice or apple cider, cornstarch, bouillon granules, and reserved lime juice. Add to reserved juices in skillet. Cook and stir till thickened and bubbly, then cook and stir 2 minutes more. Stir in mint.
	● Slice chicken breasts at a 45-degree angle across the grain into about 1-inch-thick slices. Reassemble each breast on a serving platter. Spoon sauce around chicken breasts. Top with reserved lime peel strips. Garnish with fresh mint, if desired. Makes 4 servings.

If it's poultry you're craving, go for this elegant, low-fat main dish instead of that barrel of take-out fried chicken.

Cook chicken breasts.

Make sauce.

Eggplant-Chicken Parmigiana

18 Minutes
200 Calories/Serving

Nonstick spray coating **4 boned skinless chicken breast halves _or_ turkey breast tenderloin steaks (about 1 pound total)**	● Spray a 10-inch skillet with nonstick coating. Preheat skillet over medium heat. Add chicken or turkey breasts to skillet and cook about 6 minutes or till lightly browned, turning once.
4 ¼-inch-thick slices peeled eggplant **1 cup pizza sauce**	● Place _one_ eggplant slice atop _each_ chicken or turkey breast. Pour pizza sauce over all. Cook, covered, for 8 to 10 minutes or till chicken is no longer pink and eggplant is tender.
2 tablespoons grated Parmesan cheese **¼ of a 4-ounce package shredded mozzarella cheese (¼ cup)**	● Sprinkle Parmesan cheese over all. Top with mozzarella cheese. Serves 4.

Mamma mia! Look how we saved time _and_ calories in our rendition of this classic Italian dish.

First off, we skipped breading the chicken. Then we shaved even more calories by browning the chicken in a skillet sprayed with nonstick spray coating instead of adding oil. And we saved additional time by using preseasoned pizza sauce and by cooking the mixture on the range-top instead of in the oven.

Chicken-Vegetable Stir-Fry

17 Minutes
200 Calories/Serving

1 6-ounce package frozen pea pods **2 tablespoons soy sauce** **2 teaspoons cornstarch** **1 teaspoon instant chicken bouillon granules** **¾ teaspoon ground ginger** **Dash ground red pepper**	● Place frozen pea pods in a colander. Run _hot water_ over pea pods just till thawed. Drain well. Set aside. For sauce, in a small mixing bowl stir together soy sauce, cornstarch, bouillon granules, ginger, red pepper, and ¼ cup _water_. Set aside.
1 pound boned skinless chicken breast halves _or_ turkey breast tenderloin steaks **1 teaspoon cooking oil** **6 green onions, bias-sliced into 1-inch lengths (1 cup)** **1 8-ounce can sliced water chestnuts, drained**	● Slice the chicken or turkey into bite-size strips. Set aside. Preheat a wok or large skillet over high heat. Add oil. Stir-fry _half_ of the chicken or turkey in hot oil about 3 minutes or till tender. Remove from wok or skillet. Stir-fry remaining chicken or turkey and the green onions about 3 minutes. Return all chicken or turkey to the wok or skillet. Stir in water chestnuts.
1 large tomato, cut into thin wedges	● Push chicken mixture from center of wok. Stir sauce and add it to center of wok. Cook and stir till thickened and bubbly, then cook and stir 2 minutes more. Add pea pods and tomato wedges. Cook and stir about 1 minute more or till heated through. Serves 4.

Remember, even leftovers have calories. So let leftovers _be_ leftovers and save them for another meal; don't eat them while you're clearing the table.

18 Minutes
270 Calories/Serving

Turkey Curry

1½ cups quick-cooking rice	● Cook rice according to package directions. Set aside.
1 medium apple, cored and cut into thin wedges (1½ cups) 1 medium onion, chopped (½ cup) 2 to 2½ teaspoons curry powder ½ teaspoon bottled minced garlic *or* ⅛ teaspoon garlic powder ⅛ teaspoon ground cinnamon	● Meanwhile, in a medium saucepan cook apple, onion, curry powder, garlic, cinnamon, and ¼ teaspoon *salt* in 2 tablespoons *water* till onion is tender. Remove saucepan from heat.
1 tablespoon all-purpose flour 1 8-ounce carton plain low-fat yogurt 8 ounces fully cooked turkey breast portion, chopped (2 cups) ½ cup chicken broth ¼ cup raisins	● Stir flour into yogurt, then stir into onion mixture. Stir in turkey, chicken broth, and raisins. Cook and stir over medium heat till thickened and bubbly, then cook and stir 1 minute more.
2 tablespoons chopped dry roasted peanuts	● Serve over hot cooked rice. Sprinkle with peanuts. Makes 5 servings.

Unlike some curry dishes that are spicy hot, this one, because of its apples and raisins, has a delicate, sweet flavor.

18 Minutes
230 Calories/Serving

Shrimp Creole

1 cup quick-cooking rice 2 tablespoons dried parsley flakes	● Cook rice according to package directions. Stir in parsley flakes. Set aside.
1 12-ounce can (1½ cups) vegetable juice cocktail 4 green onions, sliced (½ cup) 2 teaspoons Worcestershire sauce ½ teaspoon sugar ½ teaspoon dried thyme, crushed ¼ teaspoon ground red pepper	● Meanwhile, for creole sauce, in a medium saucepan stir together vegetable juice cocktail, green onions, Worcestershire sauce, sugar, thyme, and red pepper. Simmer, uncovered, for 5 minutes.
4 teaspoons cornstarch 1 tablespoon cold water 1 pound frozen shelled shrimp	● Combine cornstarch and water. Stir into creole sauce. Rinse shrimp if icy. Add frozen shrimp to creole sauce. Cook and stir over medium-high heat to boiling. Reduce heat and simmer, uncovered, for 1 to 3 minutes or till shrimp is tender, stirring occasionally. Serve over hot cooked rice. Serves 4.

We streamlined this Cajun specialty by cooking the frozen shrimp in the creole sauce instead of precooking it separately. (If your frozen shrimp is icy, rinse it under hot water so the ice can't dilute the sauce.)

Sweet-and-Sour Meatballs

28 Minutes
340 Calories/Serving

1 beaten egg
¼ cup fine dry bread crumbs
1 tablespoon soy sauce
¼ teaspoon garlic powder
¾ pound lean ground pork
　Nonstick spray coating

● In a medium mixing bowl combine egg, bread crumbs, soy sauce, and garlic powder. Add pork and mix well. Shape pork mixture into 24 meatballs.
　Spray a medium skillet with nonstick coating. Preheat skillet over medium heat. Add meatballs to skillet and cook about 15 minutes or till no pink remains, gently turning meatballs occasionally to brown evenly. Drain on paper towels.

1 cup water
2 cups loose-pack frozen broccoli, baby carrots, and water chestnuts
1 cup quick-cooking rice

● Meanwhile, in a medium saucepan bring water to boiling. Add frozen vegetables and cook, covered, about 5 minutes or till vegetables are crisp-tender. Remove saucepan from heat and stir in *uncooked* rice. Cover and set aside.

1½ cups apple juice *or* apple cider
2 tablespoons cornstarch
2 tablespoons vinegar
2 teaspoons brown sugar
⅛ teaspoon ground ginger
　Dash salt

● In another medium saucepan stir together apple juice or apple cider, cornstarch, vinegar, brown sugar, ginger, and salt. Cook and stir till thickened and bubbly. Gently stir in meatballs. Cook and stir about 2 minutes more or till heated through.
　Serve meatballs over rice-vegetable mixture. Makes 4 servings.

Our Test Kitchen used this little tip for quickly shaping these meatballs: On waxed paper, we patted the meat mixture into a 6x4-inch rectangle. Then we cut the rectangle into 1-inch cubes and rolled each cube into a ball. For larger or smaller meatballs, vary the thickness of the rectangle and the size of the cubes.

Gingersnap Pork Chops

25 Minutes
260 Calories/Serving

4 ¾-inch-thick pork loin chops, trimmed of fat (about 1¾ pounds total)

● Place chops on the unheated rack of a broiler pan. Broil 3 to 4 inches from the heat for 15 to 17 minutes or till no pink remains, turning once.

Make life easy! Line your broiler pan with foil and spray the unheated rack with nonstick spray coating. The rack will clean up easily in hot, soapy water, and to clean the pan you can just lift out the foil liner, wad it up, and give it a toss.

2 tablespoons chopped onion
1 tablespoon margarine *or* butter
½ cup water
2 gingersnap cookies, crushed (2 tablespoons)
2 tablespoons raisins
1 tablespoon red wine vinegar
½ teaspoon instant beef bouillon granules
Dash pepper

● Meanwhile, for gravy, in a small saucepan cook onion in margarine or butter till tender but not brown. Stir in water, crushed cookies, raisins, vinegar, bouillon granules, and pepper. Cook and stir till thickened and bubbly. Serve gravy over chops. Makes 4 servings.

Apple-Yogurt-Sauced Lamb Chops

21 Minutes
210 Calories/Serving

6 ¾-inch-thick lamb rib *or* loin chops, trimmed of fat (about 1¼ pounds total)

● Place chops on the unheated rack of a broiler pan. Broil 3 to 4 inches from the heat to desired doneness, turning once (allow 10 to 12 minutes total time for medium and 14 to 16 minutes total time for well-done).

We call for either lamb rib chops or loin chops, but there is a difference between the two. Loin chops include a portion of the tenderloin, as well as the loin eye muscle, and are identified by the T-shaped backbone. Rib chops have a rib bone and the rib eye muscle, but no tenderloin. The taste for either cut is the same.

½ cup plain low-fat yogurt
1 tablespoon all-purpose flour
1 small apple, cored and finely chopped (½ cup)
1 teaspoon sugar
⅛ teaspoon ground cinnamon

● Meanwhile, for sauce, in a small saucepan combine yogurt and flour. Stir in apple, sugar, and cinnamon. Cook and stir till thickened and bubbly, then cook and stir 1 minute more. (If sauce is too thick, stir in 1 to 2 teaspoons hot water.)

Apple slices (optional)

● Serve sauce over chops. Garnish with apple slices, if desired. Makes 3 servings.

Think Thin!

Because losing weight is a mental as well as a physical challenge, you may need to revamp some of your eating habits and attitudes about food before shedding pounds. As you diet, give these simple tips a try:

● Eat four, five, or even six *mini*-meals a day instead of three regular-size meals. The practice of eating three meals a day is based not on nutritional principles, but on convenience. Some dieters find that they don't get as hungry between meals if they eat mini-meals throughout the day. But others find it more difficult to keep their calorie counts under control with the mini-meals. Try both systems and use the one that works for you and your life-style. *Whichever* system you choose though, it's important to keep your eating times regularly scheduled.

● Eat slowly, cutting and chewing each bite deliberately. (You might even try putting your fork down between bites.) This gives your brain time to acknowledge the food you're eating and to stop sending the messages that make you think you're hungry. By eating slowly and stopping when you're full, you're practicing one of the best dieting exercises—pushing yourself away from the table!

● Change your snacking habits. Replace cookies, candy, and chips—all high-calorie snacks—with fresh fruit and vegetables. These healthy snacks will satisfy your craving to munch, but contribute fewer calories. (And don't buy high-calorie snacks to have around "just in case guests drop by.")

● If you find yourself nibbling junk food while you're watching television, find something to keep your hands busy. Try giving yourself a manicure, working crossword puzzles, doing needlework, or balancing your checkbook.

● Do your grocery shopping *after* eating to reduce the urge to buy junk food on impulse. Make a shopping list before you go, and stick to it.

Cheese-Sauced Schnitzel

25 Minutes
330 Calories/Serving

1 pound boneless veal leg round steak *or* sirloin steak, trimmed of fat **Pepper (optional)**	● Cut veal into 4 pieces. Place 1 piece of veal between 2 pieces of clear plastic wrap. Working from the center to the edges, pound with a meat mallet to ¼-inch thickness. Repeat with remaining veal. Sprinkle lightly with pepper, if desired.
⅓ cup fine dry bread crumbs **2 tablespoons grated Parmesan cheese** **2 tablespoons water** **1 egg white**	● In a shallow bowl or pie plate combine bread crumbs and Parmesan cheese. In another shallow bowl or pie plate combine water and egg white. Dip veal pieces into egg mixture, then into bread crumb mixture. Let veal stand about 10 minutes or till coating dries.
Nonstick spray coating **1 tablespoon cooking oil**	● Spray a large skillet with nonstick coating. Preheat skillet over medium heat. Add veal to skillet and cook for 4 to 5 minutes or till golden. Add cooking oil to skillet. Turn veal and cook for 3 to 4 minutes more or till golden. Remove from skillet. Keep warm.
¾ cup skim milk **1 teaspoon cornstarch** **½ teaspoon instant chicken bouillon granules** **2 ounces Neufchâtel cheese, cut into ½-inch pieces**	● For sauce, stir together milk, cornstarch, and bouillon granules. Add to skillet. Cook and stir till thickened and bubbly, scraping to loosen browned bits from bottom of skillet. Add Neufchâtel cheese. Cook and stir about 2 minutes more or till cheese melts. Serve sauce with veal. Makes 4 servings.

Cut your preparation time and work by looking for packages labeled veal scaloppine in the meat section of your supermarket. The veal in these packages is cut ¼ inch thick, so you can omit the pounding step.

Salmon-Sauced Vermicelli

25 Minutes
370 Calories/Serving

6 ounces vermicelli
1 7¾-ounce can red salmon

● Cook vermicelli according to package directions. Drain well and keep warm. Meanwhile, drain salmon. Remove skin and bones and discard. Break salmon into large chunks (see photo, below). Set aside.

You get a triple dose of calcium from this recipe (352 milligrams per serving) because of three excellent sources: Swiss cheese, canned salmon, and skim milk.

1 cup frozen peas
2 green onions, sliced
　(⅓ cup)
1 tablespoon margarine *or* butter
2 teaspoons cornstarch
½ teaspoon dried dillweed
1¼ cups skim milk
2 slices process Swiss cheese, torn (2 ounces)

● For sauce, in a medium saucepan cook peas and green onions in margarine or butter till crisp-tender. Stir in cornstarch, dillweed, ¼ teaspoon *salt*, and ¼ teaspoon *pepper*. Add milk all at once. Cook and stir till thickened and bubbly. Add cheese, stirring to melt.

1 2½-ounce jar sliced mushrooms, drained
1 2-ounce jar sliced pimiento, drained

● Stir mushrooms, pimiento, and salmon into sauce. Cook and stir till heated through. Toss sauce with vermicelli. Makes 4 servings.

Drain the canned salmon well, then turn it out onto a small plate. Using your fingers, separate the salmon into sections. Carefully remove and discard the skin, any bones, and the cartilage. Break the salmon into large chunks and set it aside until you're ready to use it.

Poached Fish With Vegetables

25 Minutes
170 Calories/Serving

1 16-ounce package frozen fish fillets
1 medium yellow summer squash, halved lengthwise and sliced ¼ inch thick (2 cups)
1 4-ounce can sliced mushrooms, drained
½ of a small onion, sliced and separated into rings
1 8-ounce can tomato sauce
1 tablespoon cornstarch
Several dashes bottled hot pepper sauce

● Place frozen fish block in a large skillet. Add squash, mushrooms, and onion rings.
  In a small mixing bowl stir together tomato sauce, cornstarch, and hot pepper sauce. Pour tomato mixture over fish and vegetables in skillet.
  Bring to boiling. Reduce heat and simmer, covered, for 15 to 20 minutes or till fish tests done (see information at right).

Properly cooked fish has an opaque appearance, with juices that are milky white. When tested with a table fork, the flesh in the thickest part of the fish flakes easily and separates readily from the bones, if present.
  Undercooked fish has a translucent appearance, with juices that are clear and watery. When tested with a fork, the flesh is firm and doesn't flake easily.

1 pound fresh spinach

● Meanwhile, wash spinach thoroughly. In a large saucepan, cook spinach, covered, with just the water that clings to the leaves. When steam forms, reduce heat and uncover. Cook and toss lightly about 3 minutes or till spinach just begins to wilt. Drain well.

● Serve fish and vegetable mixture over bed of spinach. Makes 4 servings.

Broccoli-Tuna Casserole

22 Minutes
320 Calories/Serving

5 ounces cavatelli (2 cups)
1 10-ounce package frozen cut broccoli

● Cook cavatelli according to package directions, adding frozen broccoli the last 5 to 7 minutes of cooking. Drain well. Return cavatelli and broccoli to saucepan.

Our taste panel gave this homey, stove-top casserole the highest compliment a low-calorie dish can receive: "It doesn't taste diet!"

1 10¾-ounce can condensed cream of chicken soup
1 8-ounce can sliced water chestnuts, drained
½ cup plain low-fat yogurt
½ of a 4-ounce package shredded cheddar cheese (½ cup)
1 teaspoon Worcestershire sauce
¼ teaspoon garlic powder
1 9¼-ounce can tuna (water pack), drained and flaked

● Meanwhile, in a medium mixing bowl stir together soup, water chestnuts, yogurt, cheese, Worcestershire sauce, and garlic powder. Stir soup mixture into saucepan with drained cavatelli and broccoli. Fold in tuna. Cook over medium-low heat about 5 minutes or till heated through, stirring occasionally. Makes 5 servings.

Seafood Potpie

45 Minutes
390 Calories/Serving

½ of a 15-ounce package folded refrigerated unbaked piecrusts (1 crust)

● Let the piecrust stand at room temperature for 20 minutes according to package directions.

Break through the flaky piecrust and discover a shipload of clams, shrimp, and vegetables.

1 6½-ounce can minced clams
1 16-ounce package loose-pack frozen broccoli, cauliflower, and carrots
1 2-ounce can mushroom stems and pieces, drained
1 tablespoon dried minced onion
1 teaspoon instant chicken bouillon granules
¼ teaspoon dried thyme, crushed

● Meanwhile, drain clams, reserving the liquid. In a medium saucepan stir together the frozen vegetables, mushrooms, dried minced onion, bouillon granules, thyme, and reserved clam liquid. Bring to boiling. Reduce heat and simmer, covered, about 5 minutes or till vegetables are crisp-tender.

¾ cup skim milk
2 tablespoons cornstarch
1 6-ounce package frozen cooked shrimp

● In a small mixing bowl combine milk and cornstarch. Stir into saucepan. Cook and stir till thickened and bubbly. Stir shrimp and clams into saucepan. Transfer to a 1½-quart casserole.

● Place piecrust atop casserole. Turn edges under. Flute edges. Prick crust with the tines of a fork.
  Bake in a 450° oven for 18 to 20 minutes or till crust is golden. Serves 4.

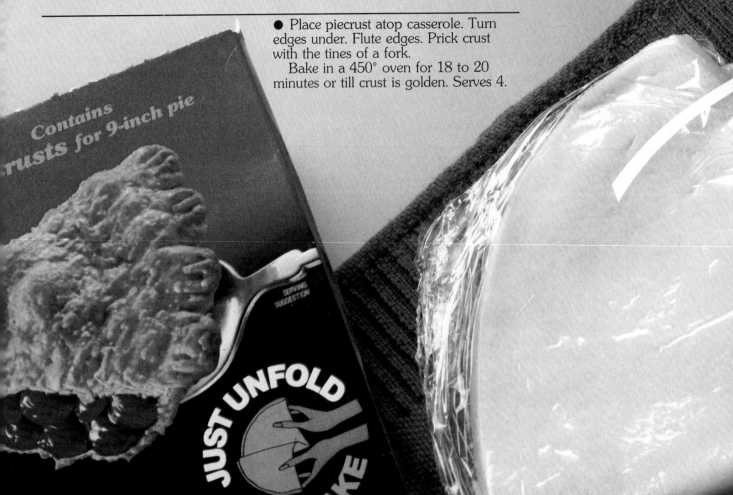

Add seafood to thickened vegetable mixture.

Top with crust.

Beefy Tex-Mex Dinner

39 Minutes
340 Calories/Serving

1 pound lean ground beef 1 medium onion, chopped (½ cup)	● In a medium skillet cook ground beef and onion till meat is brown and onion is tender. Drain off fat.
2 10-ounce cans tomatoes with green chili peppers 1 16-ounce can dark red kidney beans, drained 1 cup water ⅔ cup long grain rice 1 teaspoon chili powder ¼ teaspoon ground cumin ½ of a 4-ounce package shredded cheddar cheese (½ cup)	● Stir *undrained* tomatoes with green chili peppers, kidney beans, water, rice, chili powder, and cumin into skillet. Bring to boiling. Reduce heat and simmer, covered, about 20 minutes or till rice is tender. Sprinkle with cheese. Makes 6 servings.

No need to cook the rice first: it cooks with the other ingredients in this fuss-free skillet meal.

Vegetable-Taco Puff

27 Minutes
270 Calories/Serving

Nonstick spray coating 2 eggs ¾ cup skim milk ¾ cup all-purpose flour	● Spray the bottom and sides of a 10-inch ovenproof skillet with nonstick coating. Set aside. For puff, in a medium mixing bowl combine eggs, milk, and flour. Beat with a rotary beater till smooth. Pour egg mixture into prepared skillet. Bake in a 425° oven for 15 to 18 minutes or till puffed and golden.
½ of a 16-ounce package (about 2 cups) loose- pack frozen broccoli, corn, and peppers	● Meanwhile, place frozen vegetables in a colander. Run *hot water* over vegetables just till thawed. Drain well.
¾ pound lean ground beef 1 medium onion, chopped (½ cup) 1 16-ounce jar taco sauce	● In a large saucepan cook ground beef and onion till meat is brown and onion is tender. Drain off fat. Stir in taco sauce and drained vegetables. Cook, covered, about 3 minutes or till vegetables are crisp-tender.
½ of a 4-ounce package shredded mozzarella cheese (½ cup)	● Spoon meat-vegetable mixture atop cooked puff. Top with cheese. Cut into wedges to serve. Makes 6 servings.

Get a head start on meal preparation by stocking your shelves with products that are already shredded, chopped, or crumbed. They may cost a little more, but when you're racing the clock, every second counts.

Hamburger-Zucchini Casserole

30 Minutes
260 Calories/Serving

¾ **pound lean ground beef**
1 **medium onion, chopped (½ cup)**
½ **teaspoon bottled minced garlic** *or* **⅛ teaspoon garlic powder**

● In a large skillet cook ground beef, onion, and garlic till meat is brown and onion is tender. Drain off fat.

1 **8-ounce can tomato sauce**
1 **7½-ounce can tomatoes, cut up**
1 **teaspoon Worcestershire sauce**
½ **teaspoon dried oregano, crushed**
¼ **teaspoon ground cinnamon**
3 **medium zucchini, cut into ¼-inch-thick slices (about 6 cups)**
⅓ **cup grated Parmesan cheese**
¼ **cup bulgur**

● Stir tomato sauce, *undrained* tomatoes, Worcestershire sauce, oregano, and cinnamon into skillet. Bring to boiling. Reduce heat and simmer, uncovered, for 5 minutes. Stir in zucchini, *2 tablespoons* Parmesan cheese, and bulgur.
    Cover and cook over medium-low heat for 10 to 15 minutes or till zucchini is tender, stirring occasionally. Sprinkle with the remaining Parmesan cheese. Makes 4 servings.

Speed up your cooking by using bottled minced garlic or garlic powder instead of mincing a clove of fresh garlic.
    Look for the bottled garlic on a shelf in the produce section of your grocery store. You'll find garlic powder with the other spices and seasonings.

Is It Low Calorie?

When it comes to food labels, diet terms have specific meanings. Since 1979, low-calorie packaged foods (excluding meat and poultry products) have had to meet Food and Drug Administration regulations. Here's how the FDA defines the terms you find on food labels:

● A *low-calorie* food or beverage cannot contain more than 40 calories per serving and must bear complete nutrition labeling.
● *Reduced-calorie* foods must have at least one-third fewer calories than and be similar in taste, smell, and texture to the standard version of the same food. Reduced-calorie foods also must include nutrition labeling.
● The term *light* (*lite*) on products can mean anything from a lighter color or texture to less sodium or fat, or fewer calories. The FDA has no legal definition for light. But the U.S. Department of Agriculture, which regulates meat and poultry products, does have specific guidelines. Light (and leaner and lower-fat) meat or poultry must have at least 25 percent less fat than like products. *Or,* light may refer to a 25 percent reduction in sodium, calories, or breading; the label will tell you where the reduction is. (The use of the term light on frozen-dinner or entrée packages is not restricted.)

Shepherd's Pie Skillet

22 Minutes
220 Calories/Serving

1 pound ground raw turkey	● In a large skillet cook turkey till brown. Drain off fat, if necessary.
2 10-ounce cans tomatoes with green chili peppers ½ of a 6-ounce can (⅓ cup) tomato paste 1 tablespoon dried minced onion 2 teaspoons chili powder ¼ teaspoon garlic powder 1 9-ounce package frozen cut green beans	● Stir *undrained* tomatoes with green chili peppers, tomato paste, onion, chili powder, and garlic powder into skillet. Break up frozen green beans while still in the package. Stir beans into skillet. Bring to boiling. Reduce heat and simmer, covered, for 5 to 10 minutes or till beans are crisp-tender.
Packaged instant mashed potatoes (enough for 4 servings) ⅓ cup plain low-fat yogurt	● Meanwhile, prepare instant mashed potatoes according to package directions, *except* reduce water to 1 cup. Stir yogurt into prepared mashed potatoes.
¼ of a 4-ounce package shredded cheddar cheese (¼ cup)	● Drop potatoes into mounds atop turkey mixture. Sprinkle with cheese. Makes 6 servings.

Avoid preparing one meal for the dieter in your family and another for everybody else by serving this home-style skillet supper. It's guaranteed to satisfy the whole family's appetites.

Turkey Sausage And Kraut Supper

32 Minutes
320 Calories/Serving

2 medium potatoes, sliced ¼ inch thick (2 cups) 2 medium carrots, thinly sliced (1 cup) 1 medium onion, chopped (½ cup) 2 teaspoons instant beef bouillon granules 1 teaspoon bottled minced garlic *or* ¼ teaspoon garlic powder ¾ pound fully cooked smoked turkey sausage, sliced ½ inch thick 1 16-ounce can sauerkraut with caraway seed, drained	● In a medium skillet combine potatoes, carrots, onion, bouillon granules, garlic, and ¾ cup *water*. Bring to boiling. Reduce heat and simmer, covered, for 10 minutes. Stir turkey sausage and sauerkraut into skillet. Cover and cook for 5 to 10 minutes more or till turkey sausage is heated through and vegetables are tender.
½ cup Thousand Island reduced-calorie salad dressing	● Stir salad dressing into skillet and heat through. Makes 4 servings.

You'd never guess that this hearty skillet dinner belongs on a dieter's table—and neither will your dinner guests!

Shepherd's Pie Skillet

Turkey-Carrot Puffs

35 Minutes
240 Calories/Serving

1 cup skim milk
1 tablespoon dried minced
     onion
1 tablespoon cornstarch
1 teaspoon instant chicken
     bouillon granules
¼ teaspoon dried thyme,
     crushed
2 slices process Swiss
     cheese, torn (2 ounces)
1 8-ounce can diced carrots,
     drained
4 ounces fully cooked
     turkey breast portion,
     chopped (1 cup)

2 egg whites
½ cup reduced-calorie
     mayonnaise *or* salad
     dressing
½ teaspoon prepared
     mustard
2 tablespoons grated
     Parmesan cheese

● In a medium saucepan combine milk, onion, cornstarch, bouillon granules, thyme, and ¼ teaspoon *pepper.* Cook and stir till thickened and bubbly. Add Swiss cheese, stirring to melt.

Stir carrots and chopped turkey into saucepan. Spoon turkey mixture into four 10-ounce custard cups or individual casseroles. Set aside.

● Beat egg whites with an electric mixer on high speed till stiff peaks form (tips stand straight). Fold mayonnaise or salad dressing and mustard into stiffly beaten egg whites (see photo, below). Spoon egg white mixture atop turkey mixture in custard cups or casseroles. Sprinkle with Parmesan cheese.

● Bake in a 400° oven about 15 minutes or till egg white mixture is golden. Serve immediately. Serves 4.

Prove to any doubters that dieting *doesn't* mean eating skimpy portions of "rabbit food" by serving these hearty individual casseroles.

To fold the mayonnaise and mustard into the stiffly beaten egg whites, cut through the mixture with a rubber spatula. Scrape across the bottom of the bowl, then bring the spatula up and over the egg whites, just under the surface.

Repeat this circular down-across-up-and-over motion, turning the bowl frequently for even distribution.

Do not stir the mayonnaise and mustard into the egg whites. Stirring would break down the fluffy consistency of the egg whites.

Hot-and-Spicy Turkey Pie

40 Minutes
370 Calories/Serving

¾ cup chicken broth
1 stalk celery, sliced (½ cup)
1 medium onion, chopped (½ cup)
½ cup salsa
4 teaspoons cornstarch
12 ounces fully cooked turkey breast portion, chopped (3 cups)
1 8-ounce can whole kernel corn, drained

● In a medium saucepan combine chicken broth, celery, and onion. Bring to boiling. Reduce heat and simmer, covered, for 3 to 4 minutes or till vegetables are crisp-tender. *Do not drain.*
  In a small mixing bowl stir together salsa and cornstarch. Add to saucepan along with turkey and corn. Cook and stir till thickened and bubbly, then cook and stir 2 minutes more. Pour turkey mixture into an 8x8x2-inch baking dish. Set turkey mixture aside.

1 8½-ounce package corn muffin mix
2 4-ounce cans diced green chili peppers, drained
½ of a 4-ounce package shredded cheddar cheese (½ cup)

● Prepare corn muffin mix according to package directions. Stir in chili peppers and cheese.
  Spread corn muffin mixture evenly over turkey mixture. Bake in a 425° oven about 20 minutes or till golden brown. Makes 6 servings.

You control the thermostat in this casserole. Just choose the salsa hotness level you prefer.

15-Minute Chowder

Extra Fast

15 Minutes
380 Calories/Serving

2 cups frozen loose-pack hash brown potatoes with onions and peppers
1 10-ounce package frozen peas and carrots
2 teaspoons instant chicken bouillon granules

● In a large saucepan combine hash brown potatoes, frozen peas and carrots, bouillon granules, and 1 cup *water*. Bring to boiling. Reduce heat and simmer, covered, for 5 minutes.

1 13-ounce can (1⅔ cups) evaporated skim milk
1 tablespoon cornstarch
Several dashes bottled hot pepper sauce
12 ounces fully cooked smoked turkey sausage, sliced (3 cups)

● Stir together evaporated skim milk, cornstarch, and hot pepper sauce. Add to saucepan all at once. Cook and stir till thickened and bubbly. Stir in turkey sausage and cook about 2 minutes more or till heated through. Makes 4 servings.

Plan several days' meals at once so you can buy all your groceries in just one supermarket trip. After all, a trip to the pantry takes a lot less time than another trip to the store.

Turkey Pocket Sandwiches

Extra Fast
13 Minutes
310 Calories/Serving

4 ounces fully cooked
    turkey breast portion,
    chopped (1 cup)
1 cup preshredded fresh
    cabbage
1 small apple, cored and
    chopped (¾ cup)
½ of a 4-ounce package
    shredded cheddar
    cheese (½ cup)
⅓ cup plain low-fat yogurt
⅓ cup reduced-calorie
    mayonnaise *or* salad
    dressing
2 teaspoons prepared
    mustard
2 large whole wheat pita
    bread rounds, halved
    crosswise

● In a medium mixing bowl stir together turkey, cabbage, apple, cheese, yogurt, mayonnaise or salad dressing, and mustard. Spoon turkey mixture into pita halves. Makes 4 servings.

Wrap both hands around this pita sandwich. It's stuffed with turkey, cheese, and crunchy cabbage and apple.

Turkey Patties With Lemon Sauce

24 Minutes
150 Calories/Serving

½ teaspoon dried basil,
    crushed
¼ teaspoon onion powder
1 pound ground raw turkey
    Nonstick spray coating

● In a medium mixing bowl stir together basil and onion powder. Add ground turkey and mix well. Shape turkey mixture into four ½-inch-thick patties.
    Spray the unheated rack of a broiler pan with nonstick spray coating. Place patties on rack. Broil 3 to 4 inches from the heat for 12 to 14 minutes or till well-done, turning once.

1 tablespoon all-purpose
    flour
½ teaspoon instant chicken
    bouillon granules
½ teaspoon finely shredded
    lemon peel
⅔ cup skim milk
1 tablespoon snipped dried
    chives

● Meanwhile, for lemon sauce, in a small saucepan combine flour, bouillon granules, and lemon peel. Add milk all at once. Cook and stir till thickened and bubbly, then cook and stir 1 minute more. Stir in chives. Spoon sauce over turkey patties. Makes 4 servings.

Take a hike! No matter how careful you are with your diet, you can't be your healthiest without exercise. In addition to trimming flab, exercise strengthens your heart and lungs, lowers your blood pressure, and may even reduce stress and your blood cholesterol level.

Cajun-Spiced Burgers

22 Minutes
270 Calories/Serving

1 beaten egg
⅓ cup soft bread crumbs
1 teaspoon Cajun Seasoning
1 pound lean ground beef
4 lettuce leaves
4 tomato slices

● In a medium mixing bowl combine egg, bread crumbs, and Cajun Seasoning. Add ground beef and mix well. Shape mixture into four ¾-inch-thick patties.

Place patties on unheated rack of a broiler pan. Broil 3 to 4 inches from the heat to desired doneness, turning once (allow about 12 minutes for medium).

Serve patties on lettuce leaves with tomato slices. Makes 4 servings.

Cajun Seasoning: In a small mixing bowl stir together ½ teaspoon *garlic salt,* ½ teaspoon *white pepper,* ½ teaspoon *black pepper,* ½ teaspoon ground *red pepper,* and ¼ teaspoon *dry mustard.* Makes 2¼ teaspoons.

Use the leftover Cajun Seasoning to pep up pork chops, a pork roast, or fish fillets.

Onion-Dipped Beef Sandwiches

Extra Fast
11 Minutes
210 Calories/Serving

2 French-style rolls (about 8 inches long)
1 tablespoon horseradish mustard

● Cut rolls in half crosswise, then halve lengthwise. Spread cut sides with horseradish mustard. Set aside.

Use leftover roast beef or buy deli roast beef for these hurry-up sandwiches.

1 cup water
1 single-serving-size envelope *instant* onion soup mix
1 teaspoon Worcestershire sauce
8 ounces thinly sliced cooked beef

● In a medium saucepan combine water, soup mix, and Worcestershire sauce. Bring to boiling. Add beef slices to soup mixture. Cook and stir about 1 minute or till meat is heated through.

Remove meat from soup mixture and drain. Place meat on bottom halves of rolls. Top with roll tops. Serve each sandwich with some of the hot soup mixture. Makes 4 servings.

Sprouts
Green pepper
Turkey
Cream cheese mixture

Cheese
Turkey
Cream cheese mixture

Cream cheese mixture

16 Minutes
340 Calories/Serving

Turkey Club Sandwiches

¼ cup reduced-calorie soft-style cream cheese
2 teaspoons horseradish mustard

● In a small mixing bowl stir together cream cheese and horseradish mustard.

12 slices thinly sliced firm-texture whole wheat *or* rye bread
8 ounces sliced turkey luncheon meat (8 round slices)
4 ounces thinly sliced Monterey Jack cheese with jalapeño peppers (4 slices)

● Spread cream cheese mixture on *one* side of *each* bread slice. Top cream cheese side of *four* of the bread slices with *half* of the turkey luncheon meat and *all* of the cheese.

Monterey Jack, unlike other cheeses, isn't available sliced in packages at the grocery store. If you'd like to buy some already sliced, check your local deli.

1 medium green pepper, seeded and cut into rings
¼ cup alfalfa sprouts

● Top cream cheese side of *four* more of the bread slices with the remaining turkey luncheon meat, green pepper rings, and alfalfa sprouts.

● To assemble sandwiches, stack *one* turkey-green-pepper-sprout layer atop *each* turkey-cheese layer. Top each stack with a remaining bread slice, cream cheese side down.

● To serve, cut each sandwich diagonally into quarters and secure with toothpicks. Makes 4 servings.

Chunky Ground-Beef Stew

30 Minutes
300 Calories/Serving

1 **pound lean ground beef** ½ **teaspoon bottled minced garlic** *or* ⅛ **teaspoon garlic powder**	● In a 4½-quart Dutch oven cook ground beef and garlic till meat is brown (stir only occasionally to keep meat in large chunks). Drain off fat.
1 **28-ounce can tomatoes, cut up** 1 **16-ounce package loose-pack frozen broccoli, cauliflower, and carrots** 1 **6-ounce can tomato juice** 1 **1¼-ounce envelope** *regular* **onion soup mix** 1 **bay leaf**	● Stir *undrained* tomatoes, frozen vegetables, tomato juice, soup mix, bay leaf, and ¼ teaspoon *pepper* into Dutch oven. Bring to boiling. Reduce heat and simmer, covered, for 5 minutes.
1 **14-ounce package frozen cottage fried potatoes**	● Stir in frozen potatoes. Return to boiling. Reduce heat and simmer, covered, for 7 to 10 minutes or till potatoes are heated through. Remove bay leaf. Makes 6 servings.

When you're dieting, be aware of the differences in the fat content (and therefore the calorie count) of ground beef. *Extra lean* ground beef contains about 15 percent fat (85 percent lean) and 214 calories for a 4-ounce serving. *Lean* ground beef contains about 25 percent fat (75 percent lean) and 261 calories for a 4-ounce serving. *Regular* ground beef chalks up about 30 percent fat (70 percent lean) and 284 calories for a 4-ounce serving.

Creamy Turkey And Rice Soup

Extra Fast
20 Minutes
190 Calories/Serving

1 **medium onion, chopped (½ cup)** ½ **teaspoon bottled minced garlic** *or* ⅛ **teaspoon garlic powder** 2 **tablespoons cornstarch** ¼ **teaspoon dried marjoram, crushed** ¼ **teaspoon dried basil, crushed** 2½ **cups skim milk** 1 **14½-ounce can chicken broth**	● In a 3-quart saucepan cook onion and garlic in 2 tablespoons *water* till tender. Stir in cornstarch, marjoram, basil, ¼ teaspoon *salt,* and ¼ teaspoon *pepper.* Add milk and chicken broth all at once. Cook and stir till thickened and bubbly, then cook and stir for 2 minutes more.
1 **10-ounce package frozen rice with peas and mushrooms** 6 **ounces fully cooked turkey breast portion, chopped (1½ cups)** 12 **cherry tomatoes, halved (1 cup)**	● Stir frozen rice and chopped turkey into saucepan. Cook for 6 to 8 minutes or till heated through, stirring occasionally. Stir in cherry tomato halves. Serve immediately. Makes 5 servings.

Keep instant chicken bouillon granules on your cupboard shelf as a quick-and-easy substitute for canned chicken broth. Dissolve 2 teaspoons granules in 1¾ cups water to match the volume of a 14½-ounce can of broth.

Turkey Taco Salad

20 Minutes
240 Calories/Serving

6 ounces fully cooked
   turkey breast portion,
   chopped (1½ cups)
1 cup salsa

● In a medium saucepan stir together turkey and salsa. Cook about 8 minutes or till heated through, stirring occasionally.

4 cups torn lettuce
½ of a 6-ounce package
   shredded Monterey Jack
   cheese (¾ cup)
4 cherry tomatoes,
   quartered
   Tortilla Chips

● Meanwhile, in a large salad bowl combine lettuce, shredded cheese, and tomatoes. Add turkey mixture to salad bowl and toss lightly. Arrange Tortilla Chips around the side of the salad bowl. Serve immediately. Makes 4 servings.

● **Tortilla Chips:** Stack four 8-inch *flour tortillas.* Cut the stack into quarters (see photo, below). Place tortilla wedges in a single layer on a large, ungreased baking sheet. Bake in a 350° oven for 12 to 15 minutes or till dry and crisp.

Use our low-fat, homemade Tortilla Chips instead of purchased chips when making nachos or serving salsa. Each ounce of the homemade chips contains only 1 gram of fat, compared to 6 grams of fat in each ounce of purchased chips.

Stack the flour tortillas on a cutting board and use a large knife or kitchen scissors to cut them into quarters.

Bratwurst and Split Pea Stew

45 Minutes
300 Calories/Serving

1 14½-ounce can tomatoes, cut up
2 medium potatoes, chopped (1½ cups)
1 11½-ounce can condensed split pea with ham and bacon soup
1 10-ounce package frozen whole kernel corn
1 10-ounce package frozen peas and carrots
½ pound smoked bratwurst, thinly sliced
1½ teaspoons onion powder
1½ teaspoons chili powder
½ teaspoon celery seed

● In a Dutch oven or large kettle stir together *undrained* tomatoes, potatoes, split pea soup, corn, peas and carrots, bratwurst, onion powder, chili powder, and celery seed.

Bring mixture to boiling. Reduce heat and simmer, covered, for 25 to 30 minutes or till vegetables are tender, stirring occasionally. Makes 6 servings.

Shellfish Chowder

20 Minutes
250 Calories/Serving

---

2 cups loose-pack frozen hash brown potatoes
2 cups loose-pack frozen broccoli, corn, and red peppers
1 14½-ounce can chicken broth
1 teaspoon dried basil, crushed
½ teaspoon onion salt

● In a large saucepan stir together frozen hash brown potatoes, frozen vegetables, chicken broth, basil, onion salt, and ¼ teaspoon *pepper*. Bring to boiling. Reduce heat and simmer, covered, about 5 minutes or till vegetables are crisp-tender.

---

1 6-ounce package frozen crabmeat and shrimp
2 cups skim milk
2 tablespoons all-purpose flour
1 tablespoon cooked bacon pieces

● Meanwhile, place frozen crabmeat and shrimp in a colander. Run *hot water* over seafood till thawed. Drain well.
　In a small mixing bowl stir together milk and flour. Stir into saucepan. Add drained seafood. Cook and stir till thickened and bubbly, then cook and stir 1 minute more. Sprinkle with bacon pieces. Makes 4 servings.

This minute-minding, main-dish soup is overflowing with vegetables, crabmeat, and shrimp.

Broccoli and Crab Bisque

20 Minutes
170 Calories/Serving

---

1 10-ounce package frozen chopped broccoli
2 cups chicken broth
1 2½-ounce jar sliced mushrooms, drained
½ teaspoon bottled minced garlic *or* ⅛ teaspoon garlic powder

● Place frozen broccoli in a colander. Run *hot water* over broccoli just till thawed. Drain well.
　In a large saucepan stir together chicken broth, mushrooms, garlic, and drained broccoli. Bring to boiling. Reduce heat and simmer, covered, for 5 minutes.

---

1 6-ounce package frozen crabmeat
1½ cups skim milk
4 teaspoons cornstarch
¼ teaspoon salt
¼ teaspoon dried thyme, crushed
2 slices process Swiss cheese, torn (2 ounces)

● Meanwhile, place crabmeat in a colander. Run *hot water* over crabmeat just till thawed. Drain well.
　In a small mixing bowl stir together milk, cornstarch, salt, thyme, and ⅛ teaspoon *pepper*. Stir into saucepan. Add drained crabmeat. Cook and stir till thickened and bubbly. Add cheese, stirring till cheese melts and mixture is heated through. Makes 4 servings.

A bisque is a rich, thick, velvety-smooth soup generally made with cream and shellfish. Because of its calories we eliminated the cream, but the rest of the definition is 100 percent accurate.

Tuna-Coconut Toss

30 Minutes
230 Calories/Serving

¼ cup plain low-fat
    yogurt
2 tablespoons reduced-
    calorie mayonnaise *or*
    salad dressing
1 teaspoon curry powder

● For dressing, in a small mixing bowl
stir together yogurt, mayonnaise or salad
dressing, and curry powder. Set aside.

1 12½-ounce can tuna
    (water pack), drained
1 11-ounce can pineapple
    tidbits and mandarin
    orange sections, drained
1 8-ounce can sliced water
    chestnuts, drained

● For salad, in a medium mixing bowl
stir together tuna, fruit, and water
chestnuts. Place dressing and salad
mixture, separately, into the freezer for
15 minutes to chill.

½ cup toasted coconut
    Lettuce leaves
1 to 2 tablespoons skim
    milk (optional)

● Stir the toasted coconut into the salad
mixture. Spoon onto lettuce-lined plates.
    Stir skim milk into dressing, if
necessary, to reach desired consistency.
Drizzle dressing over each salad. Makes
4 servings.

In just a few minutes you can make your own toasted coconut for this off-the-shelf main-dish salad.

    Heat and stir your coconut in a medium skillet over medium-high heat about 5 minutes or till golden. Let it cool slightly, then stir it into the chilled salad mixture.

15 Minutes
190 Calories/Serving

Oriental Turkey Salad

3 cups loose-pack frozen broccoli, baby carrots, and water chestnuts	● Place frozen vegetables in a colander. Run *hot water* over vegetables just till thawed. Drain well.
5 cups torn romaine *or* spinach **8 ounces fully cooked turkey breast portion, chopped (2 cups)**	● For salad, in a large salad bowl combine torn romaine or spinach, chopped turkey, and thawed vegetables. Set aside.
2 tablespoons salad oil **2 tablespoons vinegar** **1 tablespoon soy sauce** **1½ teaspoons sugar** **Dash ground ginger** **1 cup chow mein noodles**	● For dressing, in a screw-top jar combine salad oil, vinegar, soy sauce, sugar, and ginger. Cover and shake well. Pour dressing over salad mixture and toss lightly to coat. Add chow mein noodles. Toss again lightly. Serves 6.

Lower your sodium intake when eating Oriental by using sodium-reduced or light soy sauce.

20 Minutes
310 Calories/Serving

Scrambled Eggs and Ham

1 tablespoon margarine *or* butter
½ of a small green pepper, chopped (⅓ cup)

● In a 9-inch microwave-safe pie plate micro-cook margarine or butter, uncovered, on 100% power (high) for 40 to 60 seconds or till melted. Stir in green pepper. Cook, uncovered, on high for 2 to 3 minutes or till green pepper is tender.

8 eggs
⅓ cup skim milk
Dash pepper

● Meanwhile, in a medium mixing bowl combine eggs, milk, and pepper with a rotary beater. Stir egg mixture into green pepper in pie plate.
  Cook, uncovered, on high for 4 to 5 minutes or till eggs are almost set, pushing cooked portions to the center after 1½ minutes, then every 30 seconds.

1 11-ounce can condensed cheddar cheese soup
¾ cup skim milk
1 cup diced fully cooked ham

● In a 1½-quart microwave-safe casserole stir together condensed soup and milk. Stir in ham. Fold in the cooked egg mixture. Cook, uncovered, on high for 5 to 6 minutes or till heated through, stirring after every 2 minutes.

3 English muffins, split and toasted
Paprika

● Serve egg-ham mixture over English muffin halves. Sprinkle lightly with paprika. Makes 6 servings.

Serve this rich and cheesy main dish to Sunday brunch guests. They'll never suspect it's low calorie.

Attention, Microwave Owners

Microwave recipes were tested in countertop microwave ovens that provide 600 to 700 watts of cooking power. The cooking times are approximate because microwave ovens vary by manufacturer.

Ham and Vegetable Spuds

17 Minutes
300 Calories/Serving

2 large baking potatoes (about 7 ounces each)

● Scrub potatoes. Prick several times with a fork. Arrange potatoes on a microwave-safe plate. Micro-cook, uncovered, on 100% power (high) for 8 to 10 minutes or till tender, rearranging once. Let the potatoes stand while preparing the sauce.

½ cup desired loose-pack frozen vegetables
2 teaspoons cornstarch
1 teaspoon dried minced onion
¼ teaspoon dried marjoram, crushed
⅛ teaspoon pepper
½ cup skim milk
⅓ cup diced fully cooked ham
1 slice process Swiss cheese, torn (1 ounce)

● For sauce, place vegetables in a 1-quart microwave-safe casserole. Cook, covered, on high for 2 to 3 minutes or till vegetables are crisp-tender. Stir in cornstarch, onion, marjoram, and pepper. Stir in milk all at once.
　Cook, uncovered, on high for 2 to 3 minutes or till thickened and bubbly, stirring after every 30 seconds. Stir in ham. Cook, uncovered, on high for 1 minute. Stir in cheese till melted.

● With a hot pad, gently roll potatoes under your hand to loosen pulp. Cut a lengthwise slit in each potato, then press ends and push up.
　Transfer potatoes to individual dinner plates. Spoon vegetable-ham mixture atop potatoes. Makes 2 servings.

Organization is the key to getting meals ready on the double. Here are a few of our best hints:
1) Arrange your kitchen so you can find things quickly. Store utensils and groceries near the areas where you'll use them most often.
2) Stock duplicates of often-used utensils (measuring cups and spoons) to cut down on mid-recipe dishwashing.
3) Read recipes through and assemble everything you need before starting.

Let the spaghetti squash stand about 10 minutes after it cooks in the microwave oven. Then use a kitchen fork to shred and separate the pulp into spaghettilike strands.

Italian Meatballs With Spaghetti Squash

30 Minutes
330 Calories/Serving

1 2½- to 3-pound spaghetti
    squash
2 tablespoons water

● Halve squash lengthwise. Remove seeds from squash halves. Place squash halves, cut side down, in a shallow microwave-safe baking dish. Sprinkle with water. Cover with vented microwave-safe plastic wrap. Micro-cook on 100% power (high) for 12 to 16 minutes or till the pulp can just be pierced with a fork, giving dish a half-turn once. Let stand, covered, for 10 minutes.

Spaghetti squash, with about 34 calories per cup, is a low-calorie (as well as vitamin-rich) substitute for pasta, which has about 192 calories per cup.

1 beaten egg
2 tablespoons skim milk
¼ cup fine dry seasoned
    bread crumbs
¼ teaspoon salt
⅛ teaspoon pepper
1 pound lean ground beef

● Meanwhile, for meatballs, in a medium mixing bowl stir together egg and milk. Stir in bread crumbs, salt, and pepper. Add beef and mix well.
   Shape beef mixture into 16 meatballs. Arrange meatballs in an 8x8x2-inch microwave-safe baking dish. Cover with waxed paper. Cook on high for 5 to 7 minutes or till no pink remains, rearranging and turning meatballs over once. Drain meatballs on paper towels.

1 cup chicken broth
1 6-ounce can tomato paste
1 4-ounce can sliced
    mushrooms, drained
2 teaspoons cornstarch
¼ teaspoon dried basil,
    crushed

● In a 4-cup microwave-safe measure stir together chicken broth, tomato paste, mushrooms, cornstarch, and basil. Cook, uncovered, on high for 5 to 7 minutes or till slightly thickened and bubbly, stirring twice. Stir in meatballs. Cook for 30 seconds more.

● Meanwhile, use a fork to scrape the inside of the squash into strands (see inset photo, opposite). Pile the squash onto 4 dinner plates. Top with meatball mixture. Makes 4 servings.

Creamy Beef And Noodles

25 Minutes
290 Calories/Serving

1½ cups medium green noodles

● Cook noodles on range-top according to package directions. Drain well.

If you can't find green noodles (spinach noodles) at the supermarket, substitute regular noodles.

1 pound lean ground beef *or* pork
1 medium onion, chopped (½ cup)

● Meanwhile, crumble ground meat into a 2-quart microwave-safe casserole. Add onion. Micro-cook, covered, on 100% power (high) for 5 to 7 minutes or till no pink remains and onion is tender, stirring once. Drain off fat.

1 8-ounce can whole kernel corn, drained
1 7½-ounce can semicondensed cream of mushroom soup
½ of an 8-ounce container reduced-calorie soft-style cream cheese (½ cup)
½ teaspoon dried savory, crushed
½ teaspoon dried marjoram, crushed

● Stir corn, soup, cream cheese, savory, marjoram, cooked noodles, and ⅛ teaspoon *pepper* into casserole. Cook, covered, on high for 5 to 7 minutes or till heated through, stirring once. Set casserole aside.

2 teaspoons margarine *or* butter
¼ cup soft bread crumbs
2 tablespoons grated Parmesan cheese

● Place margarine or butter in a small microwave-safe mixing bowl. Cook, uncovered, on high for 30 to 45 seconds or till melted. Stir in bread crumbs and Parmesan cheese. Sprinkle over meat-noodle mixture. Makes 6 servings.

Spicy Italian Casserole

25 Minutes
310 Calories/Serving

5 ounces elbow macaroni (1½ cups)

● Cook macaroni on the range-top according to package directions. Drain macaroni well.

We opted for turkey sausage here because it has the same spicy seasonings as traditional sausage, but far fewer calories.

1 pound ground turkey sausage
1 15½-ounce jar meatless spaghetti sauce with tomato, garlic, and onion
¼ teaspoon crushed red pepper

● Meanwhile, crumble turkey sausage into a 2-quart microwave-safe casserole. Micro-cook, covered, on 100% power (high) for 5 to 7 minutes or till no pink remains, stirring twice. Drain off fat.
  Stir spaghetti sauce, crushed red pepper, cooked macaroni, and ¼ cup *water* into casserole. Cook, covered, on high for 4 to 6 minutes or till heated through, stirring once.

½ of a 4-ounce package shredded mozzarella cheese (½ cup)

● Sprinkle with cheese. Cook, uncovered, on high about 1 minute or till cheese melts. Makes 6 servings.

Turkey and Dumplings

25 Minutes
310 Calories/Serving

1 cup frozen mixed
    vegetables
2 tablespoons water

● Place frozen mixed vegetables and water in a 1½-quart microwave-safe casserole. Micro-cook, covered, on 100% power (high) for 2 to 3 minutes or till vegetables are crisp-tender, stirring once. Drain well.

If you don't have nonfat dry milk powder on hand, substitute 1 cup of *skim milk* and reduce the chicken broth to ⅔ cup.

½ cup nonfat dry milk
    powder
2 tablespoons cornstarch
½ teaspoon dried basil,
    crushed
1½ cups chicken broth
6 ounces fully cooked
    turkey breast portion,
    chopped (1½ cups)

● Stir dry milk powder, cornstarch, basil, and ⅛ teaspoon *pepper* into casserole. Stir in the chicken broth all at once. Cook, uncovered, on high for 4 to 6 minutes or till mixture is thickened and bubbly, stirring after *every* minute. Stir in turkey. Cook, uncovered, on high for 2 to 3 minutes more or till bubbly again, stirring once.

½ cup packaged biscuit mix
¼ of a 4-ounce package
    shredded cheddar
    cheese (¼ cup)
3 tablespoons skim milk

● Meanwhile, for dumplings, in a medium mixing bowl stir together biscuit mix and cheese. Stir in milk just till moistened. Drop dumpling mixture from a teaspoon into 4 mounds atop the hot turkey mixture (see photo, below).

● Cook, uncovered, on high for 3½ to 4 minutes or till a wooden toothpick inserted into centers of dumplings comes out clean, rotating dish once. Serves 4.

To make dumplings, drop the biscuit-mix batter by rounded teaspoons directly onto the hot turkey mixture. Micro-cook, uncovered, till a wooden toothpick inserted into the middles of the dumplings comes out clean.

Turkey-Stuffed Peppers

22 Minutes
290 Calories/Serving

¾ **pound ground turkey
    sausage**
 1 **cup canned tomato sauce
    with onion, celery, and
    green pepper**
⅓ **cup quick-cooking rice**

● For filling, crumble turkey sausage into a 1-quart microwave-safe casserole. Micro-cook, covered, on 100% power (high) for 4 to 6 minutes or till no pink remains, stirring twice. Drain off fat.

   Stir in tomato sauce. Cook, covered, on high for 2 to 3 minutes or till bubbly. Stir in *uncooked* rice. Cover and let stand for 5 minutes.

Serve the remaining tomato sauce over cooked spaghetti squash for a quick-and-easy side dish at another meal.

 2 **medium green peppers**
 2 **tablespoons water**

● Meanwhile, cut green peppers in half lengthwise. Remove and discard the seeds and membranes. Arrange the pepper halves, cut side down, in an 8x8x2-inch microwave-safe baking dish. Add water. Cover with vented microwave-safe plastic wrap.

   Cook on high for 3 to 5 minutes or till crisp-tender. Drain pepper halves, cut side down, on paper towels.

½ **of a 4-ounce package
    shredded cheddar
    cheese (½ cup)**

● Stir *half* of the cheese into the filling mixture, then spoon filling mixture into pepper halves. Arrange pepper halves in the 8x8x2-inch baking dish. Cover with waxed paper.

   Cook on high for 3 to 5 minutes or till filling is heated through, giving dish a half-turn once. Sprinkle with remaining cheese. Makes 4 servings.

20 Minutes
310 Calories/Serving

Sweet-and-Sour Turkey

1 cup quick-cooking rice

● Cook rice on the range-top according to package directions. Set aside.
    Meanwhile, preheat a 10-inch microwave browning dish on 100% power (high) for 5 minutes.

Turkey breast tenderloin steaks are very lean cuts of white meat that are skinless and boneless. There are usually two to four pieces in a one-pound package.

1 tablespoon cooking oil
8 ounces turkey breast tenderloin steaks *or* boned skinless chicken breast halves, cut into bite-size strips
1 cup frozen crinkle-cut carrots

● Add oil to browning dish, swirling to coat dish. Add turkey or chicken strips. Micro-cook, uncovered, on high for 2 to 3 minutes or till tender, stirring once. Remove turkey or chicken with a slotted spoon and set aside, reserving juices in browning dish.
    Add carrots to browning dish and cook, covered, on high for 4 to 5 minutes or till crisp-tender, stirring once.

1 19½-ounce can reduced-calorie apple pie filling
2 tablespoons vinegar
2 tablespoons soy sauce
1 teaspoon instant chicken bouillon granules
¼ teaspoon ground ginger
1 6-ounce package frozen pea pods

● Meanwhile, for sauce, in a medium mixing bowl stir together pie filling, vinegar, soy sauce, bouillon granules, and ginger. Stir sauce, pea pods, and turkey or chicken into browning dish. Cook, covered, on high for 5 to 7 minutes or till heated through, stirring once. Serve over hot cooked rice. Makes 4 servings.

Quick-Cooking Chicken

Because most people don't have a lot of leftover cooked chicken or turkey around to use in salads and casseroles, several of our recipes call for a cup measure of store-bought, fully cooked turkey breast portion. These ready-to-eat white-meat portions can be found in varying weights in your grocer's fresh-meat case. But when you've got a few minutes to spare, why not cook a chicken breast or two so you've got some cut-up cooked meat in the freezer when the need arises?

    Here are a couple of ways to turn 2 whole medium chicken breasts (1½ pounds total) into about 2 cups of chopped, cooked chicken:

● Micro-cook chicken breasts, halved lengthwise, in a microwave-safe baking dish, covered with waxed paper, on 100% power (high) for 8 to 10 minutes or till no longer pink, turning the pieces over once. Cool; skin and chop.

● Poach the chicken breasts in a 10-inch skillet in 1⅓ cups boiling water. Simmer, covered, for 18 to 20 minutes or till tender. Cool; skin and chop.

Shrimp with Beer-Cheese Sauce

27 Minutes
250 Calories/Serving

1 **10-ounce package frozen cut asparagus** 2 **tablespoons water**	● Place asparagus and water in a 1½-quart microwave-safe casserole. Micro-cook, covered, on 100% power (high) for 3 minutes.
1 **8-ounce package frozen peeled and deveined shrimp**	● Stir shrimp into casserole. Cook, covered, on high for 6 to 8 minutes or till shrimp turn pink and asparagus is crisp-tender. Remove shrimp and asparagus from casserole. Drain well and set aside.
1¼ **cups skim milk** 2 **tablespoons cornstarch** 1 **teaspoon Dijon-style mustard** ⅓ **cup light beer *or* dry white wine** 2 **slices American cheese, torn (2 ounces)**	● For sauce, in the same casserole stir together milk and cornstarch. Stir in mustard. Cook, uncovered, on high for 2 to 4 minutes or till thickened and bubbly, stirring after every minute. Stir in beer or wine and cheese, stirring till cheese melts.
2 **English muffins, split and toasted**	● Stir shrimp and asparagus into sauce. Cook, uncovered, on high about 1 minute or till heated through. 　　Serve over toasted English muffins. Makes 4 servings.

Don't let diet plans fly out the window when dinner guests arrive. Wow your company with this elegant, low-calorie dinner for four.

Glazed Pork Chop

27 Minutes
290 Calories/Serving

2 tablespoons frozen apple juice concentrate	● For glaze, in a small saucepan stir together apple juice concentrate and barbecue sauce. Heat through.
1 tablespoon hot-style barbecue sauce	

1 ¾-inch-thick pork loin chop, trimmed of fat (about 7 ounces)	● Place chop on the unheated rack of a broiler pan. Brush with some of the glaze. Broil 4 to 5 inches from the heat for 7 minutes. Turn and brush again with glaze. Broil 8 to 10 minutes more or till no pink remains. Serve with any remaining glaze. Makes 1 serving.

If you don't keep hot-style barbecue sauce around, add a dash of bottled hot pepper sauce to catsup.

Linguine Carbonara

Extra Fast

18 Minutes
340 Calories/Serving

1½ ounces linguine 1 slightly beaten egg 1 ounce fully cooked ham, cut into narrow strips 1 teaspoon dried parsley flakes Dash pepper	● Cook the linguine according to package directions. Meanwhile, in a small mixing bowl combine beaten egg, ham strips, parsley flakes, and pepper.

2 tablespoons grated Parmesan cheese	● Immediately drain linguine, then return it to the hot saucepan. Add egg mixture. Toss to coat. Add Parmesan cheese and toss again (see photo, right). Serve immediately. Makes 1 serving.

As you toss the egg mixture and Parmesan cheese with the hot cooked linguine, the egg thickens and cooks, helping to make a rich and delicious coating that clings to the pasta.

Extra Fast

14 Minutes
320 Calories/Serving

Pita Pizza For One

3 ounces lean ground beef
2 tablespoons chopped
    green pepper

2 tablespoons canned
    chopped mushrooms
2 tablespoons pizza sauce
⅛ teaspoon dried oregano,
    crushed
1 large pita bread round,
    split horizontally
  Crushed red pepper
    (optional)
1 tablespoon shredded
    mozzarella cheese

● In a small skillet cook ground beef and green pepper till meat is brown and green pepper is tender. Drain off fat.

● Stir mushrooms, pizza sauce, and oregano into skillet. Cook and stir about 1 minute or till meat mixture is heated through. Spread meat mixture over *one* pita bread half. (Store remaining pita bread half for another use.) Sprinkle with crushed red pepper, if desired. Top with shredded cheese.
  Place pita bread on a baking sheet. Broil 3 to 4 inches from heat about 2 minutes or till cheese melts. Serves 1.

Sometimes the best buys in the meat case are in larger packages. To make the most of your purchase, divide the meat into recipe-size portions and freeze for future use.

Extra Fast

15 Minutes
310 Calories/Serving

Chili Con Carne

1 cup hot-style tomato juice
½ of an 8-ounce can (½ cup)
    red kidney beans,
    drained
½ cup cubed cooked beef
2 teaspoons dried minced
    onion
½ teaspoon chili powder
⅛ teaspoon ground cumin
⅛ teaspoon bottled minced
    garlic *or* dash garlic
    powder

● In a small saucepan stir together tomato juice, kidney beans, cooked beef, onion, chili powder, cumin, and garlic.
  Bring to boiling. Reduce heat and simmer, uncovered, about 10 minutes or till slightly thickened, stirring occasionally. Makes 1 serving.

Remember: You can always substitute regular tomato juice and several dashes of bottled hot pepper sauce for the hot-style tomato juice.

Small amounts of lamb are sometimes hard to come by. For this particular recipe, our Test Kitchen suggests cutting up lamb leg sirloin chops.

Lamb-Vegetable Kabobs

Extra Fast
19 Minutes
230 Calories/Serving

1 cup quick-cooking rice
2 tablespoons dried parsley flakes
1 tablespoon lime *or* lemon juice
1 teaspoon olive oil *or* cooking oil
¼ teaspoon dried mint, crushed

● Cook rice according to package directions. Stir in parsley flakes. Set aside.

Meanwhile, in a small mixing bowl stir together lime or lemon juice, olive oil or cooking oil, and mint. Set aside.

1 small sweet red *or* green pepper, cut into 1-inch squares
¼ pound lean boneless lamb *or* beef, trimmed of fat and cut into 1-inch pieces
1 small zucchini, sliced ½ inch thick

● On two 12-inch skewers alternately thread red or green pepper squares, lamb or beef pieces, and zucchini slices.

Place skewers on the unheated rack of a broiler pan. Brush with some of the lime juice mixture. Broil 3 inches from the heat for 7 to 8 minutes or to desired doneness, turning once. Brush occasionally with the lime juice mixture. Serve kabobs over rice mixture. Serves 1.

Tarragon-Lemon Chicken Sauté

12 Minutes
130 Calories/Serving

Nonstick spray coating
1 boned skinless chicken breast half *or* turkey breast tenderloin steak (about 4 ounces)

● Spray a small skillet with nonstick coating. Preheat skillet over medium heat. Add chicken or turkey breast to skillet and cook for 8 to 10 minutes or till no longer pink, turning occasionally to brown evenly. Remove chicken or turkey breast from skillet, reserving juices. Keep chicken or turkey breast warm.

2 teaspoons lemon juice
⅛ teaspoon dried tarragon, crushed
Dash pepper

● For sauce, add lemon juice, tarragon, and pepper to reserved juice in skillet. Cook and stir till heated through, scraping to loosen browned bits from bottom of skillet. Spoon sauce over chicken or turkey breast. Serves 1.

Serve this delicate chicken dish with hot steamed broccoli or asparagus spears.

Broiled Honey Chicken

18 Minutes
140 Calories/Serving

1 tablespoon honey
¼ teaspoon finely shredded orange peel
1 teaspoon orange juice
½ teaspoon soy sauce
Dash pepper
Dash ground ginger

● For sauce, in a small mixing bowl stir together honey, orange peel, orange juice, soy sauce, pepper, and ginger.

1 boned skinless chicken breast half *or* turkey breast tenderloin steak (about 4 ounces)

● Place chicken or turkey breast on the unheated rack of a broiler pan. Brush with sauce. Broil 4 to 5 inches from the heat about 8 minutes or till chicken or turkey breast is no longer pink, turning once. Brush frequently with sauce during broiling. Makes 1 serving.

For a complete meal, serve rice pilaf with this fresh-tasting chicken breast fix-up.

Eat Out and Enjoy

Make dining out a pleasure, even if you're watching what and how much you eat. Just keep these pointers in mind:

● Arrive on time for your dinner reservation so you won't be forced to wait in the cocktail lounge, drinking and nibbling. If you want a cocktail, drink a single glass of dry wine, a spritzer, or light beer slowly so it lasts through the cocktail period and into dinner. For nonalcoholic refreshment, sip a glass of no-calorie club soda or mineral water with a wedge of lemon or lime.

● Start your meal with a broth-type soup, fresh fruit cup, or fruit or vegetable juice. Avoid creamed soups and heavily sauced pasta appetizers. When ordering a salad before dinner, ask for it minus the dressing, with a low-calorie dressing on the side, or with a lemon wedge.

● If the restaurant has a well-stocked salad bar, build your meal around an appetizing, nutritious assortment of greens and fresh vegetables. But watch out for those tempting toppings and calorie-laden dressings. Substituting a squeeze of fresh lemon or vinegar and a sprinkle of fresh pepper for the usual dressing helps you keep your salad meal within your calorie limits.

● Since serving sizes in restaurants are often very large, consider ordering a hearty appetizer (such as boiled shrimp) or a baked potato along with a small salad for your entrée. Otherwise, select your main dish from the baked, broiled, or poached poultry, fish, or lean-meat specialties. Ask how gravies and sauces are prepared. If they're made with butter or cream, request that they be served separately.

● Inquire about low-calorie, low-fat, and low-salt items if you don't see them on the menu. Fresh fruit, too, is generally available but often not listed. Many restaurants today are recognizing customer interest in light eating and are expanding their offerings.

Stacked Shrimp Sandwich

8 Minutes
270 Calories/Serving

1 ounce frozen cooked shrimp (⅓ cup)	● Place frozen shrimp in a colander. Run *hot water* over shrimp just till thawed. Drain well.
2 teaspoons reduced-calorie mayonnaise *or* salad dressing 1 teaspoon Dijon-style mustard	● Meanwhile, in a small mixing bowl stir together mayonnaise or salad dressing and mustard. Stir in drained shrimp.
2 slices mixed-grain bread 1 ¾-ounce slice Swiss cheese 4 thin cucumber slices 1 or 2 tomato slices ¼ cup alfalfa sprouts	● On one slice of bread layer cheese, shrimp mixture, cucumber, tomato, and alfalfa sprouts. Top with second slice of bread. Makes 1 serving.

Fresh tasting, flavorful, yummy. Those are just some of the words our taste panel used to describe this quick-to-fix sandwich.

Poached Salmon Amandine

10 Minutes
350 Calories/Serving

¾ cup water 1 tablespoon lemon juice 6 ounces fresh salmon *or* halibut steak, cut ¾ inch thick	● In a small skillet combine water and lemon juice. Bring to boiling. Add salmon or halibut steak to skillet. Reduce heat and simmer, covered, for 6 to 8 minutes or till fish flakes easily when tested with a fork.
½ cup loose-pack frozen French-style green beans 2 teaspoons slivered almonds ¼ cup skim milk 1 teaspoon cornstarch ¼ teaspoon instant chicken bouillon granules	● Meanwhile, place frozen green beans in a colander. Run *hot water* over green beans just till thawed. Drain well. For sauce, place almonds in a small saucepan. Cook and stir over medium heat till toasted. In a small mixing bowl combine milk, cornstarch, and bouillon granules. Add milk mixture to saucepan. Cook and stir till thickened and bubbly, then cook and stir 2 minutes more. Stir in drained green beans and heat through.
	● Transfer salmon or halibut steak to a serving plate. Spoon sauce over steak. Makes 1 serving.

Feel free to use a frozen salmon or halibut steak. Just increase the poaching time to 9 to 11 minutes.

Scallops with Mustard Sauce

2 tablespoons water
1 teaspoon coarse-grain brown mustard
½ teaspoon lemon juice

● For sauce, combine water, mustard, and lemon juice. Set aside.

No fresh scallops available in your area? Use frozen ones and let them thaw overnight in the refrigerator.

---

4 ounces fresh scallops
Nonstick spray coating
½ of a small zucchini, bias-sliced ¼ inch thick (½ cup)
1 teaspoon cooking oil

● Cut up any large scallops, if necessary. Set aside. Spray a small skillet with nonstick coating. Preheat skillet over medium heat. Add zucchini to skillet and cook and stir for 2 to 3 minutes or till tender. Remove zucchini from skillet and keep warm.
  Add oil to hot skillet, then add scallops. Cook and stir scallops for 1 to 2 minutes or till opaque. Add sauce to skillet. Cook and stir till bubbly.

---

1 tablespoon cashews

● Serve scallop mixture atop zucchini. Sprinkle with cashews. Makes 1 serving.

Skillet Okra And Vegetables

27 Minutes
100 Calories/Serving

1 16-ounce can stewed tomatoes
1 10-ounce package frozen cut okra
1 10-ounce package frozen succotash

● In a large skillet stir together *undrained* tomatoes, okra, and succotash. Season with salt and pepper.

1 tablespoon cooked bacon pieces

● Bring to boiling. Reduce heat and simmer, covered, about 20 minutes or till vegetables are crisp-tender. Sprinkle with bacon pieces. Makes 5 servings.

Look for cooked bacon pieces above the meat case at your supermarket or ask the store's meat manager where they're located.

Artichoke Hearts Au Gratin

Extra Fast
10 Minutes
80 Calories/Serving

1 9-ounce package frozen artichoke hearts

● Cook artichoke hearts according to package directions. Drain well.

1 tablespoon cornstarch
⅛ teaspoon garlic powder
¾ cup skim milk
1 4½-ounce jar sliced mushrooms, drained
2 green onions, sliced (2 tablespoons)
1 slice process Swiss cheese, torn (1 ounce)

● Meanwhile, in a medium saucepan stir together cornstarch, garlic powder, and ⅛ teaspoon *pepper*. Stir in milk, mushrooms, and green onions. Cook and stir till thickened and bubbly. Add cheese, stirring to melt. Gently stir the cooked and drained artichoke hearts into the saucepan.

4 rich round crackers, crushed (2 tablespoons)
Dash paprika

● Transfer artichoke heart mixture to a serving dish. Sprinkle with crushed crackers and paprika. Makes 4 servings.

We saved more than 15 minutes by heating this easy but elegant side dish on the stove top instead of in the oven. Apply this speedy preparation trick to some of your own favorite dishes.

Vegetable-Couscous Pilaf

¾ cup chicken *or* beef broth

1 medium carrot, sliced (½ cup)

½ of a small zucchini, thinly sliced (½ cup)

½ of a medium sweet red pepper, chopped (¼ cup)

1 2½-ounce jar sliced mushrooms, drained

½ teaspoon bottled minced garlic *or* ⅛ teaspoon garlic powder

½ teaspoon dried oregano, crushed

½ cup quick-cooking couscous

● In a medium saucepan stir together chicken or beef broth, carrot, zucchini, sweet red pepper, mushrooms, garlic, oregano, and ¼ teaspoon *salt*. Bring to boiling. Reduce heat and simmer, covered, for 3 minutes.

Remove saucepan from heat. Stir couscous into saucepan and let stand, covered, about 5 minutes or till liquid is absorbed. Makes 4 servings.

When sweet red peppers aren't available, use sweet yellow or green bell peppers instead.

25 Minutes
150 Calories/Serving

Spinach Pesto

4 ounces spaghetti *or*
    linguine

● Cook spaghetti or linguine according to package directions. Drain well and keep warm.

Definitely a forbidden food if you're watching calories, Italian pesto is a puree that traditionally includes olive oil, ground nuts, cheese, and fresh herbs. But we created a dieter's delight by skipping the nuts and oil, and emphasizing the fresh ingredients.

1½ cups torn fresh spinach
¾ cup lightly packed parsley
    sprigs, stems removed
¼ cup chicken broth
2 tablespoons grated
    Parmesan cheese
1 egg yolk
1 teaspoon dried basil,
    crushed
½ teaspoon bottled minced
    garlic *or* ⅛ teaspoon
    garlic powder
¼ teaspoon salt

● Meanwhile, for pesto, in a blender container or food processor bowl combine spinach, parsley, chicken broth, Parmesan cheese, egg yolk, basil, garlic, and salt. Cover and blend or process till smooth. (If necessary, stop machine occasionally to scrape sides.)

● Stir pesto into cooked and drained spaghetti or linguine. Return to saucepan. Cook and stir for 1 to 2 minutes or till heated through. Serves 4.

Extra Fast

15 Minutes
35 Calories/Serving

Orange-Glazed Vegetables

½ cup water
1½ cups frozen crinkle-cut
    carrots
1 6-ounce package frozen
    pea pods

● In a medium saucepan bring water to boiling. Add carrots and return to boiling. Reduce heat and simmer, covered, for 6 minutes. Add pea pods and return to boiling. Cover and simmer about 2 minutes more or till vegetables are crisp-tender. Drain well.

Pea pods and ginger add an Oriental flair to this speedy side dish.

½ teaspoon finely shredded
    orange peel
⅓ cup orange juice
1 teaspoon sugar
1 teaspoon cornstarch
¼ teaspoon ground ginger

● Meanwhile, in a small saucepan combine orange peel, orange juice, sugar, cornstarch, and ginger. Cook and stir till thickened and bubbly, then cook and stir 2 minutes more. Pour over cooked vegetables, stirring to coat. Makes 6 servings.

Sesame-Lemon Broccoli

1 **pound broccoli, cut into spears, _or_ one 10-ounce package frozen broccoli spears**	● Cook fresh broccoli, covered, in boiling water for 10 to 12 minutes or till tender. (_Or,_ if using frozen broccoli, cook spears according to package directions.) Drain well.
1 **tablespoon lemon juice** 1 **teaspoon cooking oil** ½ **teaspoon dried basil, crushed** ⅛ **teaspoon dry mustard** ⅛ **teaspoon lemon-pepper seasoning**	● Meanwhile, in a screw-top jar combine lemon juice, cooking oil, basil, mustard, and lemon-pepper seasoning. Cover and shake well to mix. Set aside.
2 **teaspoons sesame seed**	● Heat a small skillet over medium heat. Add sesame seed to skillet. Cook, stirring constantly, for 1½ to 2 minutes or till toasted (see photo, below).
	● Shake lemon mixture again just before serving. Drizzle over broccoli and toss gently. Sprinkle with toasted sesame seed. Makes 4 servings.

Add a hint of nutty flavor to any cooked vegetable with a teaspoon or two of toasted sesame seed. Toast large batches and keep them on hand in the refrigerator.

To toast sesame seed, preheat a small skillet over medium heat. Add desired amount of sesame seed to skillet and cook and stir till toasted. Watch carefully. Once the sesame seed starts to brown, it finishes toasting very quickly.

Fruit Salad With Curry Dressing

Extra Fast

14 Minutes
130 Calories/Serving

¼ cup buttermilk
2 tablespoons reduced-
   calorie mayonnaise *or*
   salad dressing
1½ teaspoons sugar
1 teaspoon curry powder

● For dressing, in a 1-cup measure combine buttermilk, mayonnaise or salad dressing, sugar, and curry powder. Cover and chill in freezer while preparing salad.

Jazz up this 14-minute fruit salad by lining your salad plates with red-tipped leaf lettuce.
   Its curly, reddish bronze tips and ruffled green leaves add color and character to the salad. And the lettuce's mild flavor is the perfect complement to the spunky, curry-flavored dressing.

1 11-ounce can pineapple
   tidbits and mandarin
   orange sections, drained
1 medium banana, sliced
   (1 cup)
1 cup seedless green
   grapes
1 small apple, cored and
   thinly sliced (about
   ¾ cup)

● For salad, in a medium mixing bowl stir together pineapple tidbits and mandarin orange sections, banana, grapes, and apple.

4 lettuce leaves

● Arrange lettuce leaves on plates. Serve salad atop lettuce. Drizzle with dressing. Makes 4 servings.

Extra Fast

15 Minutes
120 Calories/Serving

Waldorf Salad

1 medium apple, cored and
   chopped (1 cup)
1 teaspoon lemon juice
1 11-ounce can mandarin
   orange sections, drained
1 stalk celery, chopped
   (½ cup)
¼ cup raisins
2 tablespoons chopped
   walnuts
½ cup spiced apple yogurt
4 lettuce leaves

● In a medium mixing bowl toss together chopped apple and lemon juice. Stir in mandarin orange sections, celery, raisins, and walnuts. Fold in yogurt.
   Arrange lettuce leaves on plates. Serve salad atop lettuce immediately. Serves 4.

Waldorf salad is typically made with chopped apples, celery, walnuts, and a calorie-laden dressing of mayonnaise and whipping cream. Our bright and colorful variation, with a simple yogurt dressing, doesn't sacrifice anything except the calories.

Fruit Salad with Curry Dressing

Apple-Pear Salad

Extra Fast
12 Minutes
80 Calories/Serving

¼ cup plain low-fat yogurt	● In a small mixing bowl stir together yogurt and cranberry-orange sauce. Place in freezer for 10 minutes to chill.
¼ cup cranberry-orange sauce	
1 large pear	● Core and cut pear into wedges, then core and cut apple into wedges (see photo, below). Arrange pear and apple wedges on lettuce-lined plates. Dollop with chilled yogurt mixture. Serves 4.
1 large apple	
4 lettuce leaves	

Some kitchen gadgets don't save work, they only create clutter. Not true of a *wedger*. It's a nifty, timesaving utensil that cores and wedges apples and pears in one quick move. It's easy to use, easy to store, and easy to buy. Look for one in the gadget section of your supermarket.

To use a wedger, place the apple or pear on a cutting board, stem end up. Put the wedger on top of the fruit and push down firmly. You'll have nice, even wedges of fruit.

Blue Cheese And Vegetable Salad

10 Minutes
40 Calories/Serving

½ of a 16-ounce package (2 cups) loose-pack frozen zucchini, carrots, cauliflower, lima beans, and Italian beans

● Place frozen vegetables in a colander. Run *hot water* over vegetables just till thawed. Drain well.

On the table in 10 minutes flat!

2 green onions, sliced (¼ cup)
¼ cup Italian reduced-calorie salad dressing
1 2½-ounce jar sliced mushrooms, drained
1 tablespoon sliced pimiento

● Meanwhile, in a medium mixing bowl stir together green onions, salad dressing, mushrooms, and pimiento. Stir in thawed vegetables.

6 lettuce leaves
2 tablespoons crumbled blue cheese
1 tablespoon cooked bacon pieces

● Spoon vegetable mixture onto lettuce-lined plates. Sprinkle with blue cheese and bacon pieces. Makes 6 servings.

Tossed Orange Salad

12 Minutes
60 Calories/Serving

1 11-ounce can mandarin orange sections
4 cups torn lettuce, spinach, *or* romaine
3 radishes, sliced (¼ cup)
1 green onion, sliced (2 tablespoons)

● Drain mandarin orange sections, reserving 4 teaspoons juice. Set aside.
For salad, in a large salad bowl toss together torn lettuce, spinach, or romaine; radishes; green onion; and mandarin orange sections. Set aside.

Don't be caught without the makings for a tossed green salad in your crisper.
Clean and tear salad greens as soon as you get home from the supermarket, then store them in a sealed plastic bag or covered plastic container. (Place a white paper towel in the bottom to absorb excess water.) For maximum freshness, use the greens in two or three days.

⅓ cup reduced-calorie mayonnaise *or* salad dressing
¾ teaspoon sugar
⅛ teaspoon dry mustard
Few drops bottled hot pepper sauce

● For dressing, in a small mixing bowl combine mayonnaise or salad dressing, sugar, dry mustard, hot pepper sauce, and reserved mandarin orange juice.
Pour dressing over salad mixture. Toss lightly to coat. Makes 6 servings.

Skillet Fruit Dessert

12 Minutes
120 Calories/Serving

1 tablespoon brown sugar
2 teaspoons cornstarch
½ teaspoon ground cinnamon
¼ teaspoon ground nutmeg
1 16-ounce can pear slices (juice pack), drained
1 16-ounce can peach slices (juice pack)

● In a medium skillet stir together brown sugar, cornstarch, cinnamon, and nutmeg. Stir in the pear slices and *undrained* peach slices. Cook and stir till thickened and bubbly, then cook and stir for 2 minutes more.

When the urge for a sweet treat hits home, try our yummy, low-cal version of fruit crisp: spiced fruit with a crunchy topping.

¾ cup granola with cinnamon and raisins *or* wheat flakes

● Sprinkle granola or wheat flakes over fruit mixture in skillet. Makes 6 servings.

Melon Frosty

5 Minutes
110 Calories/Serving

1 cup frozen melon balls
1 cup skim milk
⅛ teaspoon ground ginger

● In a blender container combine frozen melon balls, milk, and ginger. Cover and blend till slushy.

If you're not in the mood for a dessert, try this thick, rich milk shake at breakfast. It makes a great wake-up drink.

1 cup orange *or* pineapple sherbet

● Add sherbet, a spoonful at a time, blending till well combined. (If necessary, stop machine occasionally to scrape sides.) Makes 4 servings.

Burgundy-Poached Pears

Extra Fast

17 Minutes
80 Calories/Serving

½ cup burgundy *or* rosé wine
2 tablespoons reduced-calorie orange marmalade
2 teaspoons lemon juice
⅛ teaspoon ground cinnamon
⅛ teaspoon ground nutmeg

● In a small skillet stir together burgundy or rosé wine, orange marmalade, lemon juice, cinnamon, nutmeg, and 2 tablespoons *water*. Bring to boiling.

With a show-off dessert like this, you can entertain and still stick to your diet.

2 medium pears

● Meanwhile, halve pears lengthwise, leaving stem attached to one half. Carefully remove the core from both halves, leaving the stem attached to the one half.
 Cut pear halves into thin slices, cutting almost but not quite to the stem (see photo, below). Place pear halves, skin side up, in wine mixture in skillet.
 Return mixture to boiling. Reduce heat and simmer, covered, about 7 minutes or till pears are just tender.

● Use a slotted spoon to carefully remove pears from the skillet. Place pears on individual dessert plates.
 Boil wine mixture in skillet for 3 to 4 minutes or till reduced to ¼ cup. Spoon over pears. Makes 4 servings.

When selecting pears for cooking and baking, choose firm ones that are a bit underripe.
 For this recipe, cut the pears in half lengthwise, leaving the stem attached to one half. Core both halves, again leaving the stem attached. Place the pear halves, cut side down, on a cutting board. Use a sharp knife to cut the pear halves into thin slices, cutting almost to the stem end.

Piña Colada Pudding

9 Minutes
100 Calories/Serving

1 4-serving-size package reduced-calorie *instant* vanilla pudding mix
1½ cups skim milk
1 1¼-ounce envelope whipped dessert topping mix
1 8-ounce can crushed pineapple (juice pack)
2 tablespoons coconut

● In a small mixer bowl stir together pudding mix, milk, and dessert topping mix. Beat with an electric mixer on low speed about 30 seconds or till moistened. Beat on high speed about 2 minutes more or till thickened. Fold in *undrained* pineapple.

To serve, spoon pudding mixture into individual dessert dishes. Sprinkle with coconut. Chill till dessert time. Serves 6.

15 Minutes
100 Calories/Serving

Fruit with Lemon Fluff

1 egg
1 teaspoon finely shredded
   lemon peel
2 tablespoons lemon juice

● In a small mixer bowl beat the egg, shredded lemon peel, and lemon juice with an electric mixer on high speed about 2 minutes or till foamy and well combined.

2 tablespoons sugar
½ of a 4-ounce container
   frozen whipped dessert
   topping, thawed

● Gradually beat in sugar till dissolved. Fold the lemon mixture into the thawed dessert topping.

3 cups canned mandarin
   orange sections,
   drained; sliced
   strawberries or bananas;
   seedless green grapes;
   peeled and sliced kiwi
   fruits or peaches; or
   a combination of fruits

● Spoon desired fruit into individual dessert dishes. Dollop each with lemon mixture. Makes 6 servings.

Put the frozen whipped topping in the refrigerator when you bring it home from the store. It will thaw in several hours and keep for a couple of weeks. (Whipped topping from the freezer will thaw at room temperature in about 20 minutes.)

Add sugar slowly. Beat to stiff peaks.

Simmer meringues.

Blueberry-Orange Floating Islands

Extra Fast

20 Minutes
120 Calories/Serving

3 cups hot water
2 egg whites
½ teaspoon vanilla
3 tablespoons sugar

● In a medium skillet heat the water till simmering.
 Meanwhile, for meringue, in a large mixer bowl beat egg whites and vanilla to soft peaks (tips curl over) (see top illustration, right). Gradually add sugar, beating to stiff peaks (tips stand straight) (see bottom illustration, right).

● Drop meringue by spoonfuls into simmering water, making 4 mounds. Simmer, uncovered, about 5 minutes or till meringues are set. Lift meringues from water with a slotted spoon. Drain meringues on paper towels.

1 tablespoon sugar
1½ teaspoons cornstarch
½ cup orange juice
1 cup fresh *or* frozen blueberries
1 medium banana, sliced (1 cup)

● Meanwhile, in a small saucepan stir together sugar and cornstarch. Add orange juice all at once. Cook and stir till thickened and bubbly, then cook and stir 2 minutes more. Remove saucepan from heat. Stir in blueberries and banana.

● Spoon the fruit mixture into individual dessert dishes. Top each with a meringue. Makes 4 servings.

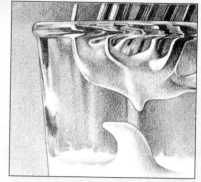

The egg white foam should be white; tips of peaks should bend over.

Egg whites should be very white and glossy; peaks should stand straight.

Snowcapped Fruit

Extra Fast
20 Minutes
110 Calories/Serving

1	tablespoon brown sugar
1	tablespoon cornstarch
¼	teaspoon ground cinnamon
1	16-ounce can peach slices (juice pack)
2	cups fresh *or* frozen red *or* black raspberries *or* blueberries

● In a medium saucepan stir together brown sugar, cornstarch, and cinnamon. Drain the peaches, reserving juice. Stir the reserved peach juice into saucepan. Cook and stir till thickened and bubbly. Stir in peach slices and berries. Cook and stir till heated through. Cover and keep warm.

True or false: Eliminating sugar is the fastest way to reduce calories.

Answer: False. Fat has the most calories of any nutrient. Reducing fat cuts calories the quickest.

3	egg whites
⅛	teaspoon cream of tartar
¼	cup sugar

● For meringue, beat egg whites and cream of tartar till soft peaks form (tips curl over). Gradually add sugar, beating till stiff peaks form (tips stand straight).

● Spoon fruit mixture into six 6-ounce custard cups. Spread meringue over fruit, swirling to make peaks in meringues.
   Place custard cups on a shallow baking pan. Bake in a 400° oven for 4 to 5 minutes or till meringues are golden. Cool slightly before serving. Serves 6.

Mixed Fruit Brûlée

22 Minutes
150 Calories/Serving

---

1 12-ounce package frozen red raspberries
½ of a 16-ounce package (2 cups) frozen unsweetened peach slices

● In an 8-inch-round baking pan stir together frozen raspberries and peach slices. Broil 4 to 5 inches from the heat for 6 to 8 minutes or till fruit is just thawed, stirring once.

Because many glass and ceramic dishes aren't broilerproof, we suggest making this mouth-watering dessert in a metal cake pan.

½ of an 8-ounce container (½ cup) reduced-calorie soft-style cream cheese
½ cup vanilla yogurt
1 tablespoon brown sugar

● Meanwhile, in a small mixer bowl beat cream cheese with an electric mixer till fluffy. Add yogurt and brown sugar. Beat till smooth.

---

2 tablespoons brown sugar

● Stir fruit once more. Spoon cream cheese mixture over fruit. Sprinkle brown sugar over cream cheese mixture.

● Broil 4 to 5 inches from the heat for 2 to 3 minutes or just till sugar melts and starts to darken. Serve immediately. Makes 6 servings.

Broccoli-Horseradish Dip

Pictured on pages 72–73.

Extra Fast

18 Minutes
18 Calories/Serving

1 10-ounce package frozen chopped broccoli	● Cook broccoli in a saucepan according to package directions. Drain well, reserving liquid. Add enough water to reserved liquid, if necessary, to make ¼ cup total.
	● In a blender container or food processor bowl combine cooked broccoli and reserved liquid. Cover and blend or process till smooth, stopping machine occasionally to scrape sides.
3 slices American cheese, torn (3 ounces) **1 tablespoon prepared horseradish** **⅛ teaspoon onion powder** **⅓ cup plain low-fat yogurt**	● Return broccoli mixture to saucepan. Stir in cheese, horseradish, and onion powder. Cook and stir over medium heat till cheese melts. Remove from heat and stir in yogurt. Return to heat and heat through, but *do not boil*.
Assorted vegetable dippers	● Transfer to a heatproof bowl. Serve with vegetable dippers. Makes about 1½ cups or 24 (1-tablespoon) servings.

Cleaning and cutting up broccoli, carrots, and cauliflower are time-consuming tasks. Check the produce section of your supermarket for pre-cut vegetables you can use for dipping.

Vegetable Dippers And Dunkers

Use low-calorie, raw vegetables for dipping into calorie-counter dips. Suggestions and their approximate calorie counts include:

● 8 carrot sticks (2½-inch)............ 12 calories
● 3 celery stalks (5-inch) ....9 calories
● ½ cup green pepper strips .... 11 calories
● 8 small cucumber slices.................4 calories
● ½ cup cauliflower flowerets .....14 calories
● ½ cup mushroom slices .... 10 calories
● 10 medium radishes......................8 calories
● ½ cup broccoli flowerets...........30 calories

18 Minutes
100 Calories/Serving

Tortilla Strips

Pictured on pages 72–73.

½ teaspoon salt
½ teaspoon ground cumin
¼ teaspoon ground red pepper
2 tablespoons margarine *or* butter, melted, *or* cooking oil
6 6-inch corn *or* flour tortillas

● In a small mixing bowl combine salt, cumin, and red pepper. Brush melted margarine or oil over *one* side of *each* tortilla, then sprinkle with salt mixture. Brush tortillas lightly to evenly distribute the salt mixture.

Try this slick idea: Use a salt shaker to sprinkle the salt mixture over the tortilla strips. It will distribute the mixture more evenly.

● Make two stacks of tortillas. Cut each stack into ½-inch strips. Place tortilla strips in a single layer on a large baking sheet. Bake in a 400° oven for 8 to 10 minutes or till crisp and lightly browned. Makes 6 servings.

Reach for these fat-reduced snacks instead of that bag of chips when you're craving something crunchy.

19 Minutes
120 Calories/Serving

Chicken Nuggets

Pictured on pages 72–73.

1 cup cornflake crumbs
2 tablespoons grated Parmesan cheese
2 teaspoons sesame seed
¼ teaspoon ground ginger
1 pound boned skinless chicken breast halves, cut into 1½-inch pieces
¼ cup skim milk *or* water

● In a medium mixing bowl stir together cornflake crumbs, Parmesan cheese, sesame seed, and ground ginger. Dip chicken pieces into skim milk or water. Coat with crumb mixture.

These crispy, bite-size chicken pieces will be a hit however you serve them—as finger food at your next party or as dinner for four.

Nonstick spray coating
⅓ cup taco sauce, salsa, *or* Dijon-style mustard

● Spray a large baking sheet with nonstick coating. Place chicken pieces in a single layer on the baking sheet. Bake in a 450° oven for 8 to 10 minutes or till no longer pink. Serve with taco sauce, salsa, or mustard. Makes 8 servings.

Broccoli-Horseradish Dip
(see recipe, page 70)

Chicken Nuggets
(see recipe, page 71)

Tortilla Strips
(see recipe, page 71)

Raspberry Spritzer
(see recipe, page 74)

Shrimp and Cucumber Cocktail

Extra Fast
15 Minutes
110 Calories/Serving

¼ cup reduced-calorie mayonnaise *or* salad dressing ¼ cup plain low-fat yogurt ½ to 1 teaspoon curry powder	● For sauce, in a small bowl combine mayonnaise or salad dressing, yogurt, and curry powder. Cover and chill.
6 cups water 1 pound fresh *or* frozen shelled large shrimp (about 24)	● Meanwhile, in a large saucepan bring water to boiling. Add fresh or frozen shrimp. Return to boiling. Reduce heat and simmer, uncovered, for 1 to 3 minutes or till shrimp turn pink, stirring occasionally. Drain and chill quickly in ice water.
1 small cucumber, thinly sliced (1 cup) Lettuce leaves	● Arrange shrimp and cucumber in lettuce-lined cocktail cups. Spoon sauce atop each serving. Makes 6 servings.

At the end of a hot summer day, serve this first-course appetizer for six as a light and refreshing dinner for four.

Raspberry Spritzers

Extra Fast
5 Minutes
100 Calories/Serving

Pictured on pages 72–73.

2 cups white grape juice 1 12-ounce package frozen red raspberries 1 tablespoon honey *or* sugar	● In a blender container combine white grape juice, raspberries, and honey or sugar. Cover and blend till smooth.
1 10-ounce bottle carbonated water Ice cubes	● Slowly add carbonated water, stirring gently to mix. Serve over ice cubes. Makes about 7 (6-ounce) servings.

Keep the ingredients for this foamy thirst quencher on hand so you can serve it to drop-in guests.

Cranberry Cooler

Extra Fast
5 Minutes
30 Calories/Serving

2 cups low-calorie cranberry juice cocktail 1 6-ounce can unsweetened pineapple juice 2 12-ounce cans low-calorie ginger ale Ice cubes	● In a large pitcher stir together cranberry juice cocktail and pineapple juice. Slowly add ginger ale, stirring gently to mix. Serve over ice cubes. Makes about 6 (8-ounce) servings.

Always add ginger ale slowly to drinks and punches so you don't lose the bubbles.

Extra Fast

5 Minutes
80 Calories/Serving

Banana Nog

1 8-ounce carton plain
   low-fat yogurt
1 cup cranberry-apple juice
1 medium banana, cut up
1 egg
  Few drops almond
   extract

● In a blender container combine yogurt, cranberry-apple juice, banana pieces, egg, and almond extract. Cover and blend till smooth.

If you have the time, cut the banana into 1-inch pieces, wrap in foil, and freeze for about an hour. Add the frozen pieces to the blender along with the ice cubes for a really frosty cold shake.

2 *or* 3 ice cubes

● With blender running, add ice cubes, one at a time, through hole in lid, blending till smooth after each addition. Makes about 6 (4-ounce) servings.

Water, Water, Everywhere

If you haven't tried any of the bottled waters now on the market, you're missing out on a real taste sensation. Like wine, each type of bottled water has its own distinct flavor, and there are lots of waters to choose from. Here are the basic types:

● *Mineral water,* often from a natural spring, contains large amounts of dissolved minerals and may or may not be carbonated. Water that comes carbonated from its underground source is labeled "naturally sparkling." If the word "natural" isn't on the label, the water probably was carbonated artificially. Mineral waters flavored with lemon, lime, and orange also are available. Mineral water, flavored or not, has no calories.

● *Club soda* (sometimes called seltzer) is carbonated tap water. Its bubbly character makes it a pleasant mixer for punches and some alcoholic drinks. It is one of the basic ingredients in most commercial soft drinks. Club soda is calorie free and also comes in various flavors.

● *Tonic water* (sometimes called quinine water) has carbonation and flavorings added. It is most often mixed with liquor and lime juice to make popular summertime drinks like gin and tonics, or vodka and tonics. There are about 65 calories per 6-ounce glass of tonic water.

50 Treats Under 100 Calories!

1. 1½ cups fresh whole strawberries dolloped with 1 tablespoon plain low-fat yogurt...*90 cal.*

2. ½ cup unsweetened applesauce sprinkled with 2 teaspoons raisins...*68 cal.*

3. 1 hard-cooked egg...*82 cal.*

4. 25 thin pretzels (½ ounce)...*55 cal.*

5. 2 cups cauliflower flowerets drizzled with 1 tablespoon creamy buttermilk reduced-calorie salad dressing...*84 cal.*

6. 1 rice cake spread with 1 tablespoon reduced-calorie soft-style cream cheese and 2 teaspoons reduced-calorie strawberry jam...*97 cal.*

7. 1 cup chopped fresh pineapple...*81 cal.*

8. 1 cup fresh blueberries...*90 cal.*

9. 3 tablespoons raisins...*79 cal.*

10. 1 fresh medium peach...*38 cal.*

11. ¼ cup vanilla ice milk sprinkled with 1 teaspoon chopped walnuts...*66 cal.*

12. Two saltine crackers (2-inch squares) spread with 2 teaspoons peanut butter...*86 cal.*

13. 1 slice frozen French toast sprinkled with 1 teaspoon powdered sugar...*95 cal.*

14. 3 fresh medium apricots...*55 cal.*

15. One 6-ounce can vegetable juice cocktail mixed with a dash bottled hot pepper sauce and a dash Worcestershire sauce. Garnish with 1 stalk celery...*38 cal.*

16. ½ of a small papaya topped with ¼ cup rainbow sherbet...*99 cal.*

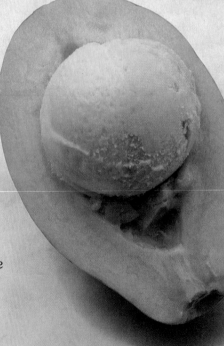

17. 8 animal crackers...*96 cal.*

18. 2 large stalks celery stuffed with 2 tablespoons (1 ounce) Camembert cheese...*99 cal.*

19. 1 medium orange, sectioned, sprinkled with 1 tablespoon coconut...*86 cal.*

20. ⅓ cup low-fat cottage cheese sprinkled with 1 tablespoon raisins...*94 cal.*

21. 2 kiwi fruits...*92 cal.*

22. 1 frozen gelatin pop bar...*35 cal.*

23. ½ of a medium grapefruit topped with 1 teaspoon honey and 1 maraschino cherry...*61 cal.*

24. ¼ of a medium acorn squash, cooked, topped with 1 tablespoon crushed pineapple...*93 cal.*

25. 4 gingersnap cookies...*96 cal.*

26. 1 large stalk celery stuffed with 1 tablespoon peanut butter...*99 cal.*

27. 4 ounces white wine mixed with 4 ounces club soda...*99 cal.*

28. 1 cup canned fruit cocktail (water pack)...*90 cal.*

29. 6 large cucumber slices (1 ounce) dipped in 2 tablespoons sour cream dip with French onion...*56 cal.*

30. Two graham crackers (2½-inch squares) spread with 2 teaspoons reduced-calorie orange marmalade...*87 cal.*

31. 1½ cups popped popcorn tossed with 1½ teaspoons melted margarine, 1½ teaspoons grated Parmesan cheese, and ¼ teaspoon chili powder...*97 cal.*

32. One 12-ounce can low-calorie root beer topped with 1 scoop (½ cup) vanilla ice milk...*99 cal.*

33. 1 cup low-calorie cranberry juice cocktail...*48 cal.*

34. 1 slice raisin bread spread with 2 teaspoons reduced-calorie soft-style cream cheese...*94 cal.*

35. 1 cup fresh whole sweet cherries...*82 cal.*

36. 2 cups diced watermelon...*84 cal.*

37. ¾ cup seedless grapes...*81 cal.*

38. 1½ cups popped popcorn tossed with 1 teaspoon melted margarine and 1 teaspoon honey...*90 cal.*

39. 2 chocolate chip cookies (2¼-inch diameter)...*99 cal.*

40. ½ of a small baked potato topped with 1 tablespoon sour-cream-and-bacon reduced-calorie salad dressing...*90 cal.*

41. 2 large dill pickles (4x1¾ inches)...*30 cal.*

42. ½ of a toasted English muffin spread with 1½ teaspoons reduced-calorie grape jelly...*94 cal.*

43. 1 cup chopped apple tossed with 1 teaspoon coconut...*94 cal.*

44. 2 plain breadsticks (7¾ inches long) dipped in 1 tablespoon soft-style cream cheese with pineapple...*91 cal.*

45. 5 vanilla wafers...*90 cal.*

46. 10 small dried peach halves...*99 cal.*

47. ½ of a cantaloupe (5-inch diameter)...*58 cal.*

48. 5 dried apricot halves spread with 1 tablespoon melted semisweet chocolate pieces...*99 cal.*

49. ½ cup apricot nectar...*68 cal.*

50. ⅓ cup lemon sherbet topped with ¼ cup sliced fresh strawberries...*94 cal.*

Slim Substitutes

Use this chart as a handy calorie-counting guide when preparing your own recipes. You'll be surprised at the calories you can save by substituting one ingredient for another.

1 cup dairy sour cream	416 calories	
1 cup plain low-fat yogurt	113 calories	**303 calories saved**
1 cup cream-style cottage cheese	239 calories	
1 cup low-fat cottage cheese	203 calories	**36 calories saved**
½ cup canned tuna (oil pack)	158 calories	
½ cup canned tuna (water pack)	126 calories	**32 calories saved**
1 cup vanilla ice cream	266 calories	
1 cup vanilla ice milk	199 calories	**67 calories saved**
1 cup whole milk	159 calories	
1 cup skim milk or buttermilk	88 calories	**71 calories saved**
1 ounce cheddar cheese	113 calories	
1 ounce mozzarella cheese	80 calories	**33 calories saved**
1 cup sweetened applesauce	232 calories	
1 cup unsweetened applesauce	100 calories	**132 calories saved**
¼ pound roasted chicken (dark meat)	234 calories	
¼ pound roasted chicken (light meat)	188 calories	**46 calories saved**
2 slices whole wheat bread	130 calories	
2 slices thinly sliced whole wheat bread	80 calories	**50 calories saved**
2 tablespoons cream cheese	106 calories	
2 tablespoons reduced-calorie soft-style cream cheese	60 calories	**46 calories saved**
1 tablespoon mayonnaise	101 calories	
1 tablespoon reduced-calorie mayonnaise	45 calories	**56 calories saved**
1 tablespoon all-purpose flour*	33 calories	
1 tablespoon cornstarch	27 calories	**6 calories saved**

*Keep in mind that to thicken sauces you use twice as much flour as cornstarch.

Index